A Personal Note From Eugenia Price

"If you are expecting order in these pages — that is, beyond the order of "the wind blowing where it listeth" — look elsewhere. What you will find here is person-to-person sharing, much as we might do were we to begin *another day* together just leafing through our Bibles.

"...Every morning we share one enormous common experience — the prospect of another day. My days, except for the differing circumstances of our lives, are not at all unlike yours: good, bad, indifferent, high, flat, bright, dark, each depending upon what we are like inside at the start of the day. One thing is sure: if living through our days depended entirely upon us, we'd be more inconsistent than the weather. But God is in charge — *if* we agree to let Him be Himself in our days."

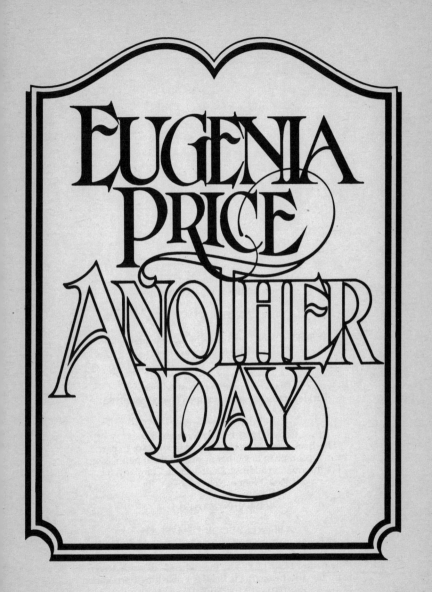

EUGENIA PRICE
ANOTHER DAY

BERKLEY BOOKS, NEW YORK

For Jimmie Harnsberger

*T*he Bible I read most often is a small, soft, leather-bound copy of the King James version that my mother once gave to my father. She, who had known Christ for most of her life, gave it to him right after his somewhat late conversion. My dad, with whom I was always unusually close, became a believer in Jesus Christ after he saw that his daughter, so like him, had finally found her own native air in the kingdom of love. I can still almost hear my father's musical voice, can almost see his eyes (mine are duplicates) dance when he said, "If my kid is so at home with Him—is so excited about Him— I want Him too."

Our house, as I was growing up, was littered with Bibles. Mother, unlike Dad and me, was a scholar. She reveled in the study of the Bible itself and Bible history. When she died recently, more than twenty years after I lost my father, I gave away crates of Bibles, maps, commentaries, and scholarly treatises that Mother had studied and studied and studied. To Dad and me, that collection of Bible history and commentary was "Mother's world," not ours. We simply were not scholars. My father wasn't even much of a reader—except for sports magazines, adventure stories, and baseball record books. I inherited my lifelong love of reading from Mother, my lifelong love of baseball from Dad. Together, in their very diverse tastes and natures, they both helped smooth my way through the early years of my Christian life. Mother's love of the Bible awakened overnight in me. And, of equal importance, my father's daring, venturesome, go the whole way or don't go at all nature (my nature to a T) held my wavering in my new faith to a minimum. At the moment of my own conversion, I abandoned myself to Christ. Anything less would have been too dull for me. God has given me what balance I have. My father and I were certainly not born with an ounce of caution or balance in the way we chose to live our lives—even if we had to team up together (and we did) to hide our real selves from Mother.

I am grateful for them both—exactly as they were. Their daughter goes on needing their traits of mind and heart.

I am still not a Bible scholar. I gave away Mother's weighty tomes, which just do not appeal to me. When I lost my laughing, deeply loving and giving father so many years ago, Mother once more proved how well she knew us both when she gave me his Bible. Stamped on its cover in gold is the name Walter Price. "Every year you live," Mother would say on my birthdays after he left us, "I see more and more of Walter Price in you." I have never and will never receive any honor to match that. Dad didn't mark his Bible at all. Like his daughter, he just wasn't a student. He'd simply open it, find something that he felt he needed that day, and promptly go about *living* what he'd found.

I readily admit that I do mark his Bible now. I'm somewhat my mother's daughter, too, and I wish I thought I managed to *live* what I find when I open Dad's Bible daily almost at random. I open it to search for a hand up for that day's needs—energy for the work ahead, comfort when my heart is heavy, guidance in making choices, stimulus in stirring up my brain so as actually to think things through, courage when I'm afraid—and often, I open it just to remind myself that there is great literature to be read. I have seldom read the Bible—Old or New Testament—without vowing to polish my own craft.

Mornings—each the beginning of another day—do not always find me first reading the Scriptures. Now and then a phone call or some immediate task to be done intervenes. That probably shouldn't be true, but it is. One thing God did for both my father and me was to make us long to be truthful, when shading the truth had, for all our years, been one of our most utilized techniques. So, I mean to, but I don't always reach first thing for the Bible. I do reach for it, though, fairly early in a new day because I don't do well otherwise.

Unlike Mother's methodical, scholarly approach, mine is to read God's Word as my dad read it—mostly at random and because I need to read. Some days when I'm working on an inspirational manuscript I think, "Oh, I've been reading the Bible all morning for my work's sake. I don't think I need to read it anymore today." Invariably, I find out in a deeper way that I must not confuse the two kinds of reading. I don't always succeed in separating them, but I try.

In these pages, you will *not* find scholarly Bible erudition. You will be sharing with me—one on one—my own daily Bible reading. I suppose in a sense I *do* study what I read. I simply have no set method of studying. I am not necessarily recommending my way, merely sharing with you a few brief insights that to me, at least, seem fresh.

Many of you, I'm grateful to say, have been reading my thoughts and concepts of God for more than thirty years. You are my friends and I am yours. Many of you have watched me grow a little with the years, shed some unneeded rigidities, experience a growing calm at the center of my being, change some priorities.

If you are expecting order in these pages—that is, beyond the order of "the wind blowing where it listeth"—look elsewhere. What you will find here is person-to-person sharing, much as we might do were we to begin *another day* together just leafing through our Bibles.

No two days are truly alike, even for the same person living them. Some days are ruled by joy, others by grief or disappointment or failure. Some are too full and some empty. Many of us are powerless to change our circumstances, but we can allow God to change us in them.

Perhaps you'd be interested to know before you begin to read that I am here trying something I've never tried. Oh, I did keep a work diary published as *Diary of a Novel,* along with the writing of my novel *Margaret's Story.* I have not attempted two unrelated books before. Until this small manuscript is finished, I will be working on these pages first at the beginning of each day and then will go to the far more wearing and difficult task of writing the second book in my Savannah quartet. Too much typing for my aging shoulders each day, but an experiment I couldn't resist. Actually, this rather odd work pattern only personalizes *Another Day.* We will not only be sharing insights on the Scriptures, you may get a little more insight into the sometimes confusing, scary work of writing a big novel. After all, I do search the Scriptures because I need God's help and believe me, He understands the anxieties, the high and low days in the life of a working novelist as He understands the anxieties and the highs and lows of your life.

Every morning we share one enormous common experience —the prospect of another day. My days, except for the differing circumstances of our lives, are not at all unlike yours: good, bad, indifferent, high, flat, bright, dark, each depending upon what we are like inside at the start of the day. One thing is sure: if living through our days depended entirely upon us, we'd be more inconsistent than the weather. But God is in charge—*if* we agree to let Him be Himself in our days.

Eugenia Price
St. Simons Island, Georgia
March 5, 1984

Old Testament

"How precious also are thy thoughts unto me, O God! how great is the sum of them! If I should count them, they are more in number than the sand: when I awake, I am still with thee."

Psalm 139:17–18

"When I awake, I am still with thee." I searched and thought a long time before choosing a theme for the first of our shared days. And during the very time spent choosing, I realized something: without having actually defined the reason, without having ever said "I have a favorite psalm," I have one. It is Psalm 139. I have used portions of it in other nonfiction books, in my novel *Maria,* and most important here, I go to it when I am dull or tired or troubled or just wondering what to read in the Bible on any day. Invariably I turn to that psalm. I have only one bookmark in the Old Testament portion of my Bible. It is at Psalm 139.

You will find other pages here based on its profound, beautifully written verses, but there can be no better way for us to begin another day together than to *stop* here—really stop—and let it soak in that the God who created mountains and winding creeks and lilacs and glossy pine needles and sky is thinking about us *today.* When we awakened *this day,* we were not alone: ". . . when I awake, I am still with thee."

I'm sure you have duties pressing you now. I have, but I've stopped long enough to take in some of the overwhelming fact that He is thinking about me this minute.

The God of the universe is thinking about you—this minute—at this beginning of another day.

"How precious . . . are thy thoughts unto me, O God!"

Psalm 139:17

How often have you heard people complain, "God just doesn't hear me anymore when I pray"? What do we really mean when we register that complaint? Do we mean that for some odd reason, the God who created and redeemed us has suddenly grown bored with hearing us call to Him? Do we mean that He is simply too busy today to bother with us? I've often heard believers say in what they evidently hope is humility, "Oh, I don't trouble the Lord with small things like that." Intended or not, such statements are an insult to the One who took the time to say from the mouth of Jesus Himself that the Father cares when even one sparrow falls to the ground.

For this day, I vow I'm going to stop every busy hour or so to remind myself that Almighty God is, in the midst of whatever occupies my mind and hands, not only thinking "thoughts unto me," He is, by that very real contact, adding to me at the center of my being.

After all, would it be possible to have direct contact with the Creator Himself and not be re-created? Not one but three repairmen are coming to make noises and talk in my house today. *Today,* with unusually hard writing to do on my novel in progress. Will God be unmindful of all that? Not on your life.

"How precious . . . are thy thoughts unto me, O God!"

"If I should count them [God's thoughts of us] they are more in number than the sand . . ."

Psalm 139:18

I happen to live on an island. I don't go to the beach anymore because it is developed almost into the sea. But more than twenty years ago, when I first moved here, my friend Joyce Blackburn and I spent hours on the then restfully empty stretches of St. Simons sand. Needless to say, we didn't try to count the grains. There are too many. We would have been overwhelmed by the effort. Anyone would.

Are God's thoughts of us that great in number? "They are more in number than the sand."

Does that sound as though God is too busy to bother with helping me figure out my bank balance? Or quiet my mind when I am anxious? Does that sound as though His time for me is limited in any way? Does it sound as though He is able to concentrate on my need of the right word for only a few minutes at a time? Does it sound as though you are entitled to only a few minutes of His time when you're afraid, as you may be right now, of what lies ahead in this day? Of what *may* lie ahead in it? Does that sound as though Almighty God is too busy with cosmic problems to realize that you are in desperate need of Him today when you have to keep that difficult appointment? When you visit that nursing home, won't He know you're there needing His own words of comfort, of understanding?

Think about it. Even those who have never seen a beach know about sand.

". . . they are *more* in number than the sand."

Psalm 139:18

❧   ❧   ❧

The same portion of Psalm 139 again? Yes. There are times when, as I read and reread these ancient lines, I feel as though an entire book could be written on this one psalm with material to spare.

The human misconception that we shouldn't "bother God" with the small incidents and problems in our daily lives is so wide that we can never dwell enough on these verses.

Think about it: the sum of God's thoughts to us is not *as great as* the sands on the beaches of the world and at the bottom of every sea. The sum of God's thoughts to us is *more* than the sands. *More.*

My dictionary gives these words as synonyms for the word "sum": aggregate, total, whole, quantity, number of. To me, this says that God's thoughts toward us are not all of one nature. They do not fall, in sum, into one high-flown, religious-sounding category. They are legion. They are inclusive. His thoughts toward us cover every need, large and small. Nothing is too enormous for Him to think about in our behalf, nothing is too small. I even pray for my favorite baseball players when they come to bat! I think in His direction, in His presence each time I step into the shower, asking that I'll be able to slow down, not hurry as I tend to do all day. I ask Him to help me enjoy the luxury of warm, soapy water long enough for the "time out" to quiet me inside after a day of leaping in my mind from one duty to another.

In that inconceivably great sum of His thoughts toward us, does He care whether or not a shower calms my thoughts, refreshes me? Yes. Yes.

"For I know the thoughts that I think toward you, saith the Lord, thoughts of peace, and not of evil . . ."

Jeremiah 29:11

꘾ ꘾ ꘾

The certainty that indeed the Lord God does think of us constantly—is able to think concentratedly about each one of us every minute of this new day and every day—has engrossed me for years. And while we can only imagine the scope of His thoughts toward us, we can know the *nature* of those thoughts.

Reread the consummately reassuring verse from Jeremiah above. I was certainly no authority on the book of Jeremiah when somewhere early in my own Christian life I found that verse. I don't memorize readily. I tend to paraphrase, but never have I forgotten the Lord's own words in that amazing verse. He actually bothered to have it set down in print so we need never wonder just what God has in mind when He thinks of you, of me. "For I know the thoughts that I think toward you, thoughts of peace, and not of evil." The hostile attitudes, criticisms, destructive gossip, and mistreatment of some Christians toward fellow human beings are not necessarily God's thoughts. "Critical Christians have made me afraid of God Himself," one young lady told me. How sad.

Who knows God's thoughts better than God Himself, who thinks them? They are "thoughts of peace, and not of evil." We, all of us, God included, think according to our nature. All we can know of God has been shown us in Jesus Christ. *Could* Jesus think thoughts of us other than peace?

"For I know the thoughts that I think toward you, saith the Lord, thoughts of peace, and not of evil, to give you *an expected end.*"

Jeremiah 29:11

At the beginning of this day, try to comprehend something of what the God who thought you up in the first place might mean by telling you that the thoughts He thinks toward you are going to give you "an expected end."

Heaven and the eternal wonder of His Presence? Is that the "expected end"? Yes. That's part of it, surely. I believe there is more.

Some of us, whether old or young, can grow too bored to go on expecting better things up ahead. I'm blessed with eternal optimism. Even when I'm exhausted from a long promotion tour, I find myself excitedly anticipating the time up ahead when I can finally begin to think again about writing another book. But what of those who have long ago stopped anticipating that "expected end"? Those who are too tired or ill or aged or strung out to think that something might be shining tomorrow? Could this verse hold new hope for people such as that?

Perhaps even more important than mere expectations—and "great expectations" do characterize a love of life—the verse holds proof that God Himself, because He knows what He is thinking, planning for us, is eager to be believed. I do believe Him. I will want to die when I can no longer write books, but I may not be able to time it right. I find comfort, assurance, *peace* in knowing that He thinks of me as He does in order to give me the *end He expects.* Even the ending of this day. Could anything possibly be better than God's expectations for us?

13

"Then shall ye call upon me, and ye shall go and pray unto me, and I will hearken unto you. And ye shall seek me, and find me, when ye shall search for me with all your heart."

Jeremiah 29:12–13

These two verses follow the verses in which God assures us that He knows what He is thinking toward us. If we grasped any of His meaning yesterday, when yesterday was "another day" to be lived through, today, in these few words, plain and clear comes the message that if we *trust* God's thoughts toward us, the ultimate human fulfillment will take place.

The ultimate human fulfillment? What is that?

It is finding God—as He is. In yesterday's verse, He assured us of His intentions toward each one of us. Today, He is saying, as I understand Him, that if we lean on the eternal value of His thoughts, His plans for us, the "expected end" will be perpetual freedom to call upon Him, knowing that He is listening. That He is already there, waiting to respond—even if we use no formed words when we seek Him. He can "hear" our thoughts.

"And it shall come to pass, that *before* they call, I will answer; and while they are yet speaking, I will hear."

Words formed into sentences for God's ear are not necessary. Words can help us concentrate, but even before we call, He has already been thinking of us. Even as we speak to Him, He is listening, giving His full attention.

"O Lord, thou hast searched me, and known me. . . . I looked on my right hand, and beheld, but there was no man that would know me . . ."

Psalm 139:1 and Psalm 142:4

❧ ❧ ❧

Once more, on this new day, I am excited with what I'm finding in Psalm 139, and a page or so beyond, in Psalm 142. Until this minute, somehow, I had never before found the connection between these two verses.

Even in a family circle (sometimes especially in a family circle) or among close friends or business associates, we all have moments, days, weeks of feeling as though no one anywhere really knows us. Knows us as we are. Not as we're supposed to be, not as we appear, but *as we are.* Those of us who happen to write books for a living or are in some other way in the public eye especially fall victim to those times when we would give almost anything if just one other person showed us that *we are known* and still loved for ourselves.

Undoubtedly, you also share these times of wishing with all your heart that just one person could see down inside you. "I looked on my right hand, and beheld, but there was no man that would know me." True. "No man [or woman] that *would* know me." No one who would even try. In those times of aloneness, it does seem now and then that no one will try. I wonder if anyone, even by trying, is *able* truly to know another person. Now, tie the two verses together for yourself. It is as authentic a test as I know as to whether or not God is a real person to us! *Everyone is known by Him.*

"Thou knowest my downsitting and mine uprising, thou understandest my thought afar off. Thou compassest my path and my lying down, and art acquainted with all my ways."

Psalm 139:2–3

Do you really believe that God knows when you sit down and when you get up?

I have no doubt but that He knows I sit too much! That He also knows that "mine uprisings" sometimes hurt because of stiff muscles. He is also "acquainted with all my ways" and so knows even better than I that such long hours spent at this typewriter or reading to keep my mind fertile affect far more about me than my aging muscles. God knows that so much time spent in my own inner world on a book like this, or the inner worlds of the characters who people my novels, too often causes me to feel strange—ill at ease, vague—when suddenly the telephone rings or I am catapulted into social contact with real people who have no idea what I've been doing or thinking. This is neither my fault nor theirs. It is simply the way things are with writers, and God understands.

The person who works all day long every day in the pressures of an executive office suite or the person who cares for and serves a family develops his or her own patterns, "ways" born of need, just as with the writer, composer, painter, teacher, physician. We all, by heredity and by the pressures of our environment, have different "ways."

In fact, our own "ways" sometimes so absorb us we totally misinterpret the needs of others. When I'm traveling, speaking, autographing in crowds, the way to show me kindness is *not* to plan one single social function outside my professional schedule. It is not being kind to me or any other person whose energies are being drained by the public to host a "small,

informal dinner where you can just relax." The Lord knows
that only privacy and a little time alone can help. Those in
public life long for time alone as deeply as those who spend
their lives in wheelchairs in nursing homes long for company!
Only God *always* understands this. Only He is "acquainted
with *all* our ways."

From morning to night—from "uprising" to "lying down"
—only He knows. But He does and we can count on that
knowing.

"Whither shall I go from thy spirit? or whither shall I flee from thy presence? If I ascend up into heaven, thou art there: if I make my bed in hell, behold, thou art there."

Psalm 139:7–8

Take whatever time is necessary, right now, to allow this to become real to you: there is nowhere—nowhere—anyone can go where God is not there too.

There is no point whatever in trying to understand how this can be. If we could understand the mysteries of God, we would have no need for faith. Faith, as I see it, simply connects us to Him in all His mystery and wonder and love.

It isn't difficult to believe that "if I ascend up into heaven, thou are there." Relating a loving God to our happy, confident moments—our "heavenly" moments—isn't particularly hard. But what about this? "If I make my bed in hell, behold, thou art there."

Does God follow us into the depths of the hell we call human tragedy or trouble? Into grief and sorrow and failure? Well, yes, unless He lied to us: "I will never leave you nor forsake you." *Never.* "Lo, I am with you always."

Even when—and I don't think I've thought enough about this line before—even when "I make my bed in hell." Even when this sorrow or loneliness or trouble is my fault! Is He there, even then? I once heard a minister advise young people not to go anywhere they couldn't take Jesus Christ. That sounds provocative, but how do we keep Him away?

"If I say, Surely the darkness shall cover me; even the night shall be light about me. Yea, the darkness hideth not from thee; but the night shineth as the day: the darkness and the light are both alike to thee."

Psalm 139:11–12

Not long ago I wrote a small book called *Getting Through the Night*, the "night" being the darkness of grief. I based it quite simply on what I see of God's way of moving us in time of blackest sorrow from the "weeping that may endure for a night" to the "joy that cometh in the morning."

I can't tell you exactly where this became clear to me, but at some point in the writing of that manuscript, I caught hold of the irrevocable fact that "the darkness and the light are both alike to thee." Because God Himself went to the life-changing trouble to become one of us in Jesus of Nazareth, He can now expect us to believe that He *knows* the difference, as we say, between day and night. The Son of God grew sleepy when He lived on earth and He slept. He also awakened to another day and found the sun up. Of course, He knew about sunrise and sleep since He created both the sun and us. But He also knew us well enough to realize that the only way we could *believe* He understood our dread of the darkness was to become one of us and share it. To limit Himself to being human. We have no excuse for disbelieving that He understands how exhausted and panic-stricken we can become in the dark.

Becoming a human being in Jesus, though, in no way changed God's knowledge and power over the universe. Jesus opened the way to our ability to lay hold of both.

"The darkness and the light are both alike to thee."

"Cause me to hear thy lovingkindness in the morning; for in thee do I trust: cause me to know the way wherein I should walk . . ."

Psalm 143:8

Each day's opening moments—when we are tossed from sleep back into consciousness—tend to be intensely personal. We have no choices to make when we sleep. But let the alarm go off or the sunlight penetrate our closed eyelids and bang—another day. We may greet it with dread, with delight, with fear, with courage, with determination, with timidity. Still the intense transition moment is there. And it is so personal because abruptly we are faced with choices.

I don't turn in that brief moment to God because I think I'm spiritual or even trying to be. I do it because I know He hasn't been asleep and knows far better than I what is ahead in this day. With me, it is merely a vital moment of recognition. I don't dive into my Bible or pray for an hour before I make coffee. I bathe, brush my teeth, make coffee, and often have stimulating or sleepy-headed talk with my friend Joyce first before concentrated time with Him. But the quality of turning to Him is not necessarily measured by length of time. Frankly, I don't count minutes when I'm consciously in touch with God. And, as you do, I usually have a long list of problems for which I need guidance, help. "For in thee do I trust: cause me to know the way wherein I should walk." He wants us to turn for help in our problems.

Today, I'm more thankful that He does.

I burst back into consciousness this morning with what to me is my most difficult kind of personal problem: I quit work yesterday with no idea where I would go in my current novel. That may not sound either personal or terrible to you. Believe me, to me it is both. I simply did not know which direction to take with the story and it made me afraid. If I went one way the book would be too long. If I took another, I'd have to come up with an entirely new ending.

I opened my Bible to where I was working on this little book yesterday. For once, my old faithful Psalm 139 seemed to calm me down only a little. So I leafed ahead to Psalm 143. In verse 8, I jumped at the lines: "Cause me to hear thy lovingkindness in the morning; for in thee do I trust: cause me to know the way wherein I should walk." Desperately, I needed to know the way in which I could manage to "walk" to the end of my story. But what caught my eye was "Cause me to hear thy lovingkindness in the morning." As usual, in my agitation, I was begging the Lord to tell me which direction to take, but I hadn't thought of listening even for a few seconds to His "lovingkindness." And so, with effort at first, I slowed my agitation, deliberately put my mind on how *kind He really is,* and then, slowly, like the sun coming up over the pine trees at the edge of the marsh behind my house, I began to find my way, to lose my fear.

Because my contract called only for a sequel to the novel *Savannah,* I was trying to cram too much material into one book! A call to my editor set me on course toward a quartet of novels—three more books instead of merely a sequel. I still don't have the solution but I now have room—space—in which to find it.

It's impossible truly to "hear" His lovingkindness in the midst of noisy agitation. Once I took time to listen, I could think straight again. I had lost my fear of failure.

"My substance was not hid from thee, when I was made in secret, and curiously wrought in the lowest parts of the earth. Thine eyes did see my substance, yet being unperfect; and in thy book all my members were written, which in continuance were fashioned, when as yet there was none of them."

Psalm 139:15–16

We live by minute and hour and second hands sweeping the face of a clock. We meet tragedy with the hopeless first minutes of crying out, "How can I live like this day after day, year after year?" Death takes a loved one. We tremble at the empty future hours, months, years. *God does not live in time.* And yet . . . and yet, He knows what it's like to be trapped in it. In Jesus He allowed Himself to be caught in time, forced to live by the rising of the sun and the going down of the sun, for thirty-three human years. And this was the same God who was there "when everything was made that was made. . . . Without Him was not anything made that was made."

It is a source of endless wonder to me that Jesus was beyond time as God, and yet, alive today, is still perfectly able to remember what it's like being us—*governed by time.* Did He really know us as the Son of God, walking the earth? Did he really have all our members written down in His book when none of them existed?

Yes. I don't understand it, either. But I believe it and fight the flying hours less and wait through the creeping hours with more peace when I remember that He does understand the effects on us of time.

"Surely thou wilt slay the wicked, O God. . . . Do not I hate them, O Lord, that hate thee? and am not I grieved with those that rise up against thee? I hate them with a perfect hatred: I count them mine enemies."

Psalm 139:19–22

Read those four verses that glower at you from my beloved Psalm 139, but whatever you do, don't stop there. Read in the New Testament what *Jesus* said about enemies: "But I say unto you, Love your enemies, bless them that curse you, do good to them that hate you, and pray for them which despitefully use you, and persecute you."

Whew! That's my honest response. For years, I hassled with those four seemingly mean-spirited verses from Psalm 139. Then I stopped hassling. When, I don't remember, but the day I began to realize that much of what seems un-Christian in the Old Testament, Jesus handled. For example, this rough treatment of our enemies. Hating enemies with a perfect hatred can be totally confusing. But Jesus came to clarify: now, *anyone* can know the *real nature* of the God of both the Old and the New Testaments. Go ahead and criticize me if you feel better doing it, but there are other references where the God of the Old Testament and the New can seem like two different Gods altogether.

The odd-appearing violence and hatred of some of God's people as recorded in the Old Testament can be devastating until and unless we catch on to the fact that He saw that ancient humankind just wasn't grasping Him *as He is,* and He did something about it. In His time, when the Father knew it was the right time, He sent His Son to wipe out our confusion.

Jesus told us to *love our enemies.* God hasn't changed. He has just been clarified by His Son.

"The Spirit of the Lord God is upon me; because the Lord hath anointed me to preach good tidings unto the meek; he hath sent me to bind up the brokenhearted, to proclaim liberty to the captives, and the opening of the prison to them that are bound; To proclaim the acceptable year of the Lord, *and the day of vengeance* of our God. . . ."

Isaiah 61:1–2

The italics are mine. If it appears to you that I am in any way downgrading the Old Testament, wait. I'm not. Rather, until I discovered that Jesus came also to clarify our understandable confusions at some of the Old Testament, I did a lot of floundering myself. At the very start of His earthly ministry, back in His hometown of Nazareth, Jesus read also from that same portion of the ancient book of Isaiah (Esaias): "The Spirit of the Lord is upon me, because he hath anointed me to preach the gospel to the poor; he hath sent me to heal the brokenhearted, to preach deliverance to the captives, and recovering of sight to the blind, to set at liberty them that are bruised. To preach the acceptable year of the Lord." That is what Jesus read in the temple that day (St. Luke 4:18–19), and then verse 20 plainly states, "And he closed the book."

Now, reread the italicized words above from Isaiah 61:1–2. They do not appear in St. Luke's account of what Jesus read in His hometown temple. Again, He was clarifying for us. Vengeance is human. Before Jesus came to live on earth, even the wisest, most devout follower of Jehovah had no way of knowing that God's way is not vengeance—for Him or for us. It is *forgiveness.* Even for our enemies.

"For the living know that they shall die: but the dead know not any thing, neither have they any more a reward; for [even] the memory of them is forgotten. Also their love, and their hatred, and their envy, is now perished; neither have they any more a portion for ever in any thing that is done under the sun."

Ecclesiastes 9:5–6

If we stop here or if we take this passage out of context, we believe exactly as I believed in the half-light days *before* I became a follower of Jesus Christ. In other words, *then,* I was convinced that once my body died, I'd be gone. Oblivion. Nothing. "The dead know not any thing."

Meeting Jesus Christ in person, recognizing Him as God's only clear revelation of Himself, His nature, His intentions toward us, changed all that. When I began to trust Him, I also began to trust what He said. And Jesus, striking life and hope and joy into the starkness of these Ecclesiastes verses, declared, "In my Father's house are many mansions: if it were not so, I would have told you. I go to prepare a place for you. And if I go and prepare a place for you, I will come again, and receive you unto myself; that where I am, there ye may be also."

Oblivion when we leave this life?

Never.

"If it were not so, I would have told you."

Clarification.

"So I returned, and considered all the oppressions that are done under the sun: and behold the tears of such as were oppressed, and they had no comforter; and on the side of their oppressors there was power; but they had no comforter."

Ecclesiastes 4:1

Here again, the "wise preacher," writer of Ecclesiastes, offered his best view of reality, throwing over that reality all the light he had. Remember, a wise man is speaking.

If one looks at oppression, bigotry, crime, suffering, and failure with the wisest *human* eye, the wise preacher was exactly right, from the reality of the natural world.

From the reality of the kingdom of love, read what Jesus had to say: "If ye love me, keep my commandments. And I will pray the Father, and he shall give you another Comforter, that he may abide with you forever; Even the Spirit of truth; whom the world cannot receive, because it seeth him not, neither knoweth him: but ye know him; for he dwelleth with you, and shall be in you. *I will not leave you comfortless:* I will come to you."

The way Jesus has worked out our comfort is to come to us Himself! There is nothing spooky or strange or weird about the Holy Spirit. He is one with the Lord we love and follow. The disciples were about to collapse with fear and grief because Jesus was leaving them—Jesus, their Master, their best Friend. Talk about grief!

The wise preacher in Ecclesiastes did not yet know of this promise. Jesus had not yet come. He has come now. He has come to be personally with us through this day, this night. Comforting us.

The Comforter is here.

"My son, if thou wilt receive my words, and hide my commandments with thee; So that thou incline thine ear unto *wisdom,* and apply thine heart to *understanding;* Yea, if thou criest after *knowledge* and liftest up thy voice for *understanding;* If thou seekest her as silver, and searchest for her as for hid treasures; Then shalt thou understand the fear of the Lord, and find the *knowledge* of God."

Proverbs 2:1–5

What does *fear* of the Lord really mean? To me, the most creative explanation is *awe.* And I learned it only minutes ago. I was checking modern translations of the word "fear" of the Lord when my best friend and housemate, Joyce Blackburn, came into my office. "My father always told me that to fear the Lord meant to be in awe of Him—who He is." I knew her father, a wonderful "character" and a man of God. His explanation suits me fine and leads directly to the point I intended to make when I copied Proverbs 2:1–5. Holding God in awe surely means, in part at least, that we are convinced that wisdom and understanding *are* God. Are as much a part of His nature as love. I have italicized in this quotation the key words: wisdom, knowledge, and understanding. If Jesus Christ and God are one, as I believe them to be, then *knowledge* and *understanding* of Him lead inevitably to both comfort and awe in His presence.

Knowledge of Christ inspires awe because to learn of Him is to learn of His holiness. Holiness evokes awe. To be in awe of God, though, is not the same as being in awe of great music or art or a vast, breathtaking river canyon. It is more. To feel awe toward all these things is surely a part of God, but when we are in need, we long for a Person. Only in Him can we find complete awe because He is singular in perfection.

Jesus said, "Learn of me." When we do, when we even begin to learn a little of what He is actually like, awe results *and* comfort. They may seem almost contradictory because we seldom think of being awe-struck and comfortable at the same time. But His knowledge of us in no way contradicts His understanding of us.

His singular holiness brings us to our knees to worship. His understanding comforts us.

"For the Lord giveth wisdom: out of his mouth cometh knowledge and understanding. . . . When wisdom entereth into thine heart, and knowledge is pleasant unto thy soul; *Discretion* shall preserve thee, understanding shall keep thee."

Proverbs 2:6,10–11

❧   ❧   ❧

When the Lord comes into a human life, wisdom comes with Him. When the Lord comes into a human life, understanding comes with Him. Even the simplest among us can begin to be comfortable, at home with great knowledge: ". . . knowledge is pleasant unto thy soul."

Undoubtedly, you, as I, have thought much about both wisdom and understanding in relation to our walk with God. But what about *discretion?*

One of my dictionary's synonyms for discretion is tact. Especially in what we say. What of the tactless, thoughtless, or insensitive Christians you know? To me, discretion is one of the keys to identification with those around us. Solomon appeared to be convinced of the need, the importance of discretion: he equated it with understanding. "Discretion shall preserve thee, understanding shall keep thee."

In the Person of our Lord are both discretion and understanding. We have direct access to both because we have direct access to Him.

"The Lord by wisdom hath founded the earth; by understanding hath he established the heavens. By his knowledge the depths are broken up, and the clouds drop down the dew."

Proverbs 3:19–20

❧ ❧ ❧

This may not seem so when a hurricane rages or a killer tornado spins out of control; when a natural tragedy strikes a loved one; when Mount St. Helens explodes over the countryside. But God is in charge. "The Lord by wisdom hath founded the earth." That fact has to include another fact: He set certain laws in motion when He did that founding. Laws of nature. These laws cannot be broken simply because a Christian lives near an exploding volcano or in the path of a storm or a flood. Christians, when trapped in an automobile struck head on by another, can and do get killed. Those two cars crashing into each other prove a basic law of physics. Inevitable consequences occur.

In the novel I'm writing each day after sharing these pages with you, I have felt exhausted and bruised and terrified and sun-burned and starved and thirsty unto death along with my characters, who survived a ghastly packet boat wreck at sea back in the year 1838. Some passengers were rescued after five days of survival on the wreckage. Most died. They all cried out to God for mercy; still almost two hundred died. I have no pat explanation. If we could explain these seeming inconsistencies, there would be no need for faith that no matter what, the Lord *is in charge.*

"Wisdom is the principal thing; therefore get wisdom: and with all thy getting get understanding."

Proverbs 4:7

❧ ❧ ❧

Wisdom alone, evidently, is not enough. Enough to appear brilliant, to attract admiration of sorts, even to prosper, but not enough to be whole.

I love the phrase "and with all thy getting get understanding." True, there is much "getting" among us. I know believers who are proud of their "much getting" even of spiritual knowledge. Proud that they've memorized so much of the Bible, that they read it through every year. Proud when someone says of them, "He or she is so spiritual." Back in the church where I grew up, there was one lady who almost never smiled. Everyone said of her, because she knew so many facts about the Bible and prayed aloud longer than anyone else, "She's so spirchul."

This "spirchul" lady ended her lonely life alone with her "much getting." People seemed never to be comfortable around her.

The truth was that she was so "spirchul" she couldn't *understand* at all when someone disagreed with her or when their life-style did not exactly match hers. I'm terribly relieved that God bothered to remind us in Proverbs 4:7 that "with all thy getting get understanding" too.

"Wisdom is the principal thing; therefore get wisdom: and with all thy getting get understanding. Exalt her, and she shall promote thee: she shall bring thee to honor, when thou dost embrace her. She shall give to thine head an ornament of grace: a crown of glory shall she deliver to thee."

Proverbs 4:7–9

Wisdom remains principal and true wisdom must lead to understanding. Anyone with a quick mind can lay hold of a lot of facts, but that isn't necessarily wisdom. Wisdom is *knowing*. And true knowing is *understanding*.

Can I achieve this kind of wisdom on my own?

Can you?

Never. Oh, there are and have been wise human beings with kind, understanding hearts who have made no profession of belief in God. No point in denying that, because it's true. Still, is it possible to "know" and to "understand" when tragedy or failure or disappointment strike? I believe not. Those of us who at least make an effort to use the minds God gave us can learn the techniques of concentration, of the retention of a certain amount of knowledge, which may often stand us in good stead.

But what about those times when there are no answers? No explanations for tragedy or heartache? That is when we need understanding beyond our own—the very wisdom and understanding of God Himself. Our inadequacy is replaced by His sufficiency.

Those aren't just words. He is enough. The pressure of trying to understand is off us and onto Him.

"Counsel is mine, and sound wisdom: I am understanding; I have strength."

Proverbs 8:14

In reading through Proverbs, I am sharing insights that have come recently and others that have been with me for years, but lately added to. This is one of those.

A long time ago, in some Bible commentary, I remember reading that "wisdom," as written of in Proverbs, is the Old Testament concept of Christ Himself. I could grasp and accept that then. I still can. Think of Jesus Christ as you read "Counsel is mine, and sound wisdom." Both belong to Him. I find it far easier to confide in Him, to seek counsel from Him, than from even the wisest human being. I write that well aware that many, many people prefer to run helter-skelter to another person for help first. A long time ago, I used to do some so-called counseling at retreats. I seldom do now. I wasn't then and am not now qualified. But even in my early, greener years as a Christian, I remember asking people who dared think that I, simply because I tried to put into words in books some of what I felt God was teaching me, could solve their problems, "Have you spoken with God about this first?"

All counsel belongs to Him. And sound wisdom. Did you notice in the proverb that after the word wisdom is a colon? That means the explanation follows. And what it says is "I *am* understanding." God doesn't just possess understanding. He *is* understanding.

"The fear of the Lord is the beginning of wisdom: and the knowledge of the holy is understanding."

Proverbs 9:10

If our fear of the Lord is awe of Him, recognition of who He really is, we are on our way toward wisdom. I once heard Dr. E. Stanley Jones speak of what he called the "holy awe" of God. There is such a thing as being "too familiar" with Jesus Christ. At first reading, this, as Dr. Jones agreed, seems a contradiction. It is and it isn't. We can, oh, we *can* tell Him anything. Anything at all—and far more than we'd dare confide to any human being. If we are sure of God's unchanging love, we can truly, to the limits of our own self-knowledge, be ourselves with Him. Stanley Jones was always quick to add, though, that if our familiarity with Him begins to slop over into glibness, "just about the time we're ready to throw an arm about His shoulder He steps back and becomes our God. Yet we can still feel free with Him."

I was struck by that when I first heard it. The effect on me holds. Perhaps it's actually easier for those of us who are, in some measure, in the public eye—who suffer from other people's images of us—to go first to God for understanding. I rather imagine it is. Christians seldom agree on what a Christian really is. Different groups have their own criteria. For that reason, I'm careful with groups. I don't need to be careful with God, though. And yet, His own holiness precludes overfamiliarity. Prevents our treating Him as though He were just a buddy. We begin to understand that the "knowledge of the holy is understanding." About Him and about us. And about other people.

"He that is void of wisdom despiseth his neighbour;
but a man of understanding holdeth his peace."

Proverbs 11:12

If we have never stopped to think—as we're attempting to do in these selected proverbs—that wisdom and understanding are irrevocably linked, this verse will sound odd. "He that is void of *wisdom* despiseth his neighbour"? Does wisdom have a lot to do with getting along with our neighbors? According to the Bible, yes.

My wise, beloved friend Lorah Plemmons, who died at age 101, before any of us was willing to let her go, "got along" with everyone, even under impossible circumstances. She was not academically educated, but she was the wisest person I ever knew, and now, after studying the verse above, I know why she was. She *understood*. She understood where we all really were on our journeys. She didn't know much about the inside of my world of publishing, but she knew me. She understood that when I seemed vague during a visit to her back porch, I was unable to get the current book off my mind. On those days, we just sat together in silence. She had worked hard all her life, but when some "highbrow" person treated her as a member of the servant class, she laughed. "That's just her way of thinking," she'd say. "I have mine and she has hers and that's all right." She understood. Therefore, she held her peace and although she was too perceptive actually to *like* everyone, she despised no one. She was truly wise.

"A talebearer revealeth secrets: but he that is of a faithful spirit concealeth the matter."

Proverbs 11:13

There is nothing new in the reminder that "a talebearer revealeth secrets." Some people seem unable *not* to drop that tantalizing bit of news, to spread the word of someone's heartache or failure or misfortune. There are even those who, if nothing new has occurred, seem unable not to make something up. I heard the other day that a tourist had come to St. Simons Island with some "news" that I am now confined to a wheelchair. I also had a sympathy letter from a dear, caring reader, who had "heard" that my best friend and housemate, Joyce Blackburn, had died.

Well, obviously someone told each of these people the happily untrue stories. The lady who wrote in such genuine sympathy because I had lost Joyce was not talebearing. She was showing understanding.

Intentionally, I picked safe examples of the damage talebearing can cause. What is important about the thirteenth verse from Proverbs 11 is that reference to a "faithful spirit." I'd never thought of that before. I'd read the verse many times, but—a "faithful spirit" can keep me from revealing secrets? Can hold my tongue, help me conceal the matter? Faithful to what? To whom? For me, it means that if I have a faithful spirit where Jesus Christ is concerned, I won't reveal a secret that might in any way hurt someone else whom He loves as much as He loves me.

When we gossip—bear tales, reveal secrets—we are not being faithful in our human spirit to the God of love. Period.

"The merciful man doeth good to his own soul: but he that is cruel troubleth his own flesh."

Proverbs 11:17

Much of what Jesus said when He lived on earth as one of us was multidimensional. Even the two simple-sounding words "Follow me" embody more than the human mind can absorb. Of course, He had spent long hours studying the Scriptures. He *is* the great clarifier of the Old Testament—the Scriptures as people knew them in His time. And yet, Jesus in no way contradicted Scriptures as He clarified. In fact, He lived them, taught them, often referred to them.

When Jesus said "The kingdom is within," was He referring to Proverb 11:17? Certainly, there is no contradiction. His words "The kingdom is within" are layered with meaning, but surely one thing He meant was that if we remain merciful, peaceful in our own hearts and minds, we help our own souls. A loving, peaceful man or woman is far more apt to be well. Medical science finally caught up to Jesus. We know that many physical diseases are consequences of bitterness, hatred, cruelty, and selfishness on the part of the ill person. Not all. But many.

"He that is cruel troubleth his own flesh." I believe that. We have all had unpleasant business or personal experiences that could have—and maybe did—make us ill. It is not what the other person does to us that counts, it is how we allow God to see us through it. If we fight back, claw, try to hurt, show cruelty, we can damage even our own flesh.

God's way isn't to be followed because He is tough. His way is simply the best way.

"The liberal soul shall be made fat: and he that watereth shall be watered also himself."

Proverbs 11:25

This in a particular sense is an elaboration on the preceding proverb. The King James version of the Bible, still my favorite because of the ring of its writing, quite comfortably used the word "fat." That was before we had grown so fat-conscious. Those of us who tend to overweight know that it not only isn't fashionable not to be thin as a rail, it draws somewhat scornful criticism. Not so in King James's time. Fat was still a delectable word. "The liberal [the giving] soul shall be made fat." The RSV declares that the liberal soul shall be "enriched." Fine, either word gets across the meaning: our own souls will be enriched, improved, shined up, elevated according to our liberality. Liberal and liberality are to me totally beautiful words. Beautiful in sound and meaning.

"He that watereth shall be watered also himself." What a lovely idea. A friend recently sent me a chrysanthemum plant. I try not to neglect it, although I'm not a gardener in any sense of the word, but I find myself enjoying that plant even more on the days I forget to water it, discover its leaves hanging and dejected, water it, wait an hour, and look again. It is like magic.

A lovely, narrow fern grows on old walls and tree boughs where I live. In dry weather, it is curled and dead-looking. Then a two- or three-hour rain comes, and the reason it is called a resurrection fern becomes plain.

"He that watereth . . ."

"The way of a fool is right in his own eyes: but he that hearkeneth unto counsel is wise."

Proverbs 12:15

You've read that verse many times, no doubt. So have I, but today it struck me in a new way—revealed a bit more to me about myself. About what comes naturally to me. Perhaps to us all.

"The way of a fool is right in his own eyes." I am what can easily be called an opinionated woman. I'll go so far as to say a highly opinionated woman. I am learning not to jump to attractive conclusions without thinking them through, but once I've decided something, I make no bones about liking my own opinion. My own opinion about politics, nuclear weapons, helping the needy, the environment, Congress, the President, social issues, art, music, literature, historical interpretations. If it's my opinion, I enjoy clinging to it. On any subject, of course, like you, I hold an opinion because I think it's right.

Am I, according to this verse from Proverbs, a fool? Perhaps. But I don't think we dare be simplistic about this verse —any verse, for that matter—because there are too many dimensions to most of what God says.

I admit to being partial to what I think is right. But in fairness to myself, I must also admit that I try, at least, to think through my opinions conscious that I'm thinking in God's presence. Now, this is not to say that He approves or agrees with me always. Certainly not with my prejudices. Still, I fail to see how we can think about the earth He created, overkill in weaponry designed to slaughter people for whom He died, the poor, art, music, or any topic without including in our thought processes what we are able to grasp of His counsel. The wise person, He tells us, "hearkeneth unto counsel."

I may not agree with you, nor you with me, but the counsel of God shouts *Love one another*. I am pigheaded only when I forget that counsel. I do get carried away with my pet opinions and forget to heed the counsel of God, but love corrects me.

"Heaviness in the heart of man maketh it stoop: but a good word maketh it glad."

Proverbs 12:25

This seems almost too obvious for a page all its own. It isn't. Especially not if thinking about this proverb causes even one of us to take time for that "good word" today.

A personal example from my own daily life: some days, especially when I'm working my way through an unusually heavy writing schedule, as now—when the unanswered, unacknowledged mail is piling up, when I'm feeling my age, or am tired and sorry for myself—I am a creature with "heaviness in the heart." This is *not* natural to me. Both my parents were upbeat people, as was my brother. I like getting up most mornings, and almost every day I'm eager to get back to the book that weariness forced me to leave the day before.

Still, there are days when requests come in such numbers I am convinced that the last thing people really want me to do is write another book! I then begin to hassle my friend Joyce, with whom I live. "If I open one more letter from some dear soul asking me to speak or inviting me to have lunch on a workday, I'll scream! When do they think I write these books they love so to read?" I can *feel* Joyce working her magic, keeping her voice calm, hoping to soothe me. Sometimes I weary her with it, but sometimes she says, "Honey, I don't know how you keep up with it all. I'm proud of you." Those "good words," especially when I honestly *haven't* fished for them in my moment of "heaviness in the heart," can "make me glad" for days! Good words are not obvious platitudes. Truly good words lift a stooping heart.

"A man shall eat good by the fruit of his mouth: but the soul of the transgressors shall eat violence."

Proverbs 13:2

Do we ever think seriously about "eating good" or "eating violence"? I've read this proverb many times. Only today, after having written yesterday's page, have I been more than mildly enlightened by it. This, of course, is one of the many reasons why reading the Scriptures can be such an ongoing experience. We seem to "understand" according to our need—on that day, at that particular reading.

Each time my friend Joyce lifts up my "stooping heart" with a "good word" of understanding, I can tell you that it helps me. My heart straightens up. The work load seems lightened even if the desk is still piled high. I'm human. I need and enjoy being understood as much as you do.

But isn't it true that while *not* thinking of herself Joyce is also benefiting Joyce? She is "eating good" of the fruit of her mouth. I'm convinced that she knows me better than I know her, although I try, but I do know her well enough to know when, humanly speaking, she would far rather "eat violence" when I complain about my work load. I complain usually because I'm tired. We'd all save ourselves and other people a lot of heartache if we'd accept the fact that weariness can distort the mind and perspective as much as alcohol! Sometimes, when Joyce is weary too, she could clobber me for even mentioning my mail. All of what I have to do I enjoy. I only need less of it. I wish I could answer all my own mail. I love to write. I have no valid reason to complain. Most of the time, though, she *chooses* to "eat good by the fruit of her mouth"— even when she'd rather not. I'm blessed.

"Only by pride cometh contention: but with the well advised is wisdom."

Proverbs 13:10

Consider the first phrase: "Only by pride cometh contention." This, of course, has to do with the well-known adage Pride goeth before a fall. Today I seem to see a bit more.

Would we be unduly proud if we were more *realistic* about ourselves and other people? Is there a difference between being proud and feeling highly fulfilled? I honestly don't know, but it bears some thought. Could it be that, at least, in our normal somewhat disparaging use of the word "proud," a proud person allows a feeling of high fulfillment to distort his or her attitudes? Does success or an enormous job accomplished cause us to feel superior to those who may not have made it yet?

"I only heard my grandparents quarrel once," a college student told me the other night. "He made the grave error of telling her that he liked a neighbor's coconut cake better than he liked my grandmother's. And zowie! Her religion sailed right out the window." A homely example, but it can be carried wherever we need to take it. That grandmother, so proud of her own cake, had probably won a lot of prizes with it in the past. She had come to feel somewhat superior about it. To her, the truth was that she baked the best coconut cakes. When Grandfather shook this truth a little, it was as though he had attacked her, so that by her injured pride "cometh contention."

None of this is to say that pride merely needs to be controlled. I doubt that it can be. What I'm wondering is this: if "only by pride cometh contention," if feelings of pride that set us apart from other human beings bring about "contention," are we following the supreme realist, Jesus Christ?

I'm all for that good feeling of fulfillment for everyone: the kind of fulfillment that can follow the baking of a cake, the cleaning of a house, the mowing of a yard, the planting of three hundred bulbs in the garden, the finish of a long manuscript on time—or the lift of heart that at times follows prayer. But I can't quite believe that fulfillment or satisfaction can rightly be equated with pride. Oh, we say, "That's a proud family" or "He's a proud man" and we often mean this as a compliment.

Maybe if whatever feeling follows a good event in our lives causes no *contention* we can know the feeling to be fulfillment and not pride. I know for a fact that a "proud" author can be a mighty haughty, contentious individual, who on occasion enjoys writing a blistering review of another writer's book. I'm certainly fulfilled when I can look at and pat a high stack of finished manuscript pages. Proud? I must check that the next time. What talent I have, *I have been given.* Talent is almost neutral where I'm concerned. The fulfillment comes from the job finished at last. At least, I think that's true. I'm going to watch myself, though, at the completion of this book and the novel I'm also writing now.

If I cause "contention" I'll know some *unrealistic* pride is the source.

"He that oppresseth the poor reproacheth his Maker: but he that honoureth him [his Maker] hath mercy on the poor."

Proverbs 14:31

I am thinking about this verse, sharing it with you at a time when my country—the world, in fact—is in deep economic trouble. Perhaps you are, as you read. We read, we hear, we see all around us proof that in certain cases the rich are getting richer and the poor, poorer. Those of us who fall somewhere in the vast middle, between the rich and the poor, need to take care.

What does it mean to oppress the poor? Whatever it means, when we do it, are we really reproaching Jesus Christ? As though we shouldn't be concerned, a wealthy Christian said to me not long ago, "But Jesus said 'the poor are always with us.' " He did, but could He have been simply stating a fact? He did a lot of fact-stating, you know. He didn't say because there is poverty, I approve of it. I don't see any hint of license to oppress the poor just because they will always be with us, do you?

"The eyes of the Lord are in every place, beholding the evil and the good."

Proverbs 15:3

❧ ❧ ❧

"The eyes of the Lord are in every place." What does that really mean? Well, to me, it does *not* mean that God is spying on our every move, our every thought, our every deed or misdeed. Some of the mail I receive indicates that there are those who think of Him that way. God spying. God playing policeman. God, sneaking around giving us no time of absolute privacy. Other mail implies that if our deeds are laudable, our gifts generous, our successes great, God is in the midst of it all. No one seems to mind if the Lord's eyes are in every place at the moment he or she is up to some commendable act. People only seem to feel uneasy when God's eyes see evil. That figures. Jesus knew that "men loved darkness rather than light because their deeds were evil."

But "the eyes of the Lord are in *every* place." In the darkness, too. "He made darkness his secret place." Every place—light, dark, shadowy, bright—is God's place. "The eyes of the Lord are in every place, beholding the evil and the good."

If we love Him, if we have entered into all that we understand of friendship with Christ, we're relieved to find Him in every place we are. In every thought, in every deed. Whether our worst or our best, He is not spying: He is redeeming.

People may misunderstand our thoughts, motives, acts. God never does. He *sees* us exactly as we are.

"A merry heart maketh a cheerful countenance: but by sorrow of the heart the spirit is broken."

Proverbs 15:13

No one questions the truth of the first phrase of this proverb. A merry heart makes for a cheerful appearance. No one questions the truth of the second phrase: ". . . by sorrow of the heart the spirit is broken."

The two phrases are different in the *effect* they have upon us, though. Are we being scolded in the second phrase? Is God asking us to do another of those seemingly impossible things?

How, when my heart is heavy with sorrow, when grief or failure or disappointment has broken my spirit, can I possibly push my aching heart to merriment so that I am cheerful to look at? "I don't want to be such depressingly bad company," a grieving gentleman wrote not long ago. "My grief over the loss of my beautiful wife just won't lessen. I notice my friends are dodging me and I don't blame them."

Does this proverb say, "Just step out there on your own and be merry, no matter how you feel?" I believe not. A lot of proverbs would drive me to despair over myself if I did not have my confidence centered in Jesus Christ Himself. Remember, one of God's numberless reasons for sending the Savior was to clarify the Old Testament for us. It is what happens to us in the world we live in that defeats us, grieves and disappoints us. But—and here is the clarifying key again—Jesus said, "Be of good cheer. I have overcome the world."

He didn't stop with that, though. He also said, "Come unto me, all ye that labour and are heavy laden, and *I* will *give* you rest."

Coming to Him redefines even the word "cheer" when our hearts are heavy and our spirits broken.

"When a man's ways please the Lord, he maketh even his enemies to be at peace with him."

Proverbs 16:7

I'm not planning to write much about this verse. If you read it a few times, I think you'll understand why.

The meaning in it is as unending as an echo. Meaning spirals away into infinity within the simple structure of these lines as do the whorls on a seashell. And only you have any means of knowing whether or not your ways truly please the Lord. Only I know about mine.

God knows, of course, but He didn't create our minds for His own amusement or His own devotion to experiment. He created our minds for *thinking.*

Do I have enemies? If so, why?

Do you have enemies? If so, why?

Could it be that somewhere in our humanly tangled "ways," even in the ways of those who try to obey, there is one secret way that does *not* please the Lord?

"The hoary head is a crown of glory, if it be found in the way of righteousness."

Proverbs 16:31

I almost missed this one. Then, when I read it more carefully, I smiled.

There is no virtue whatever, so far as I know, in *not* changing the color of one's hair, if, in the course of time, it has become "hoary." I am hoary and I happen to love it. My mother died at eighty-six with rich auburn hair—as close as her hairdresser could come to the color as I remembered it when she and I were both young. She liked it that way. "Your father didn't want me to have gray hair," she was still saying some twenty years after my father died. Her "auburn" hair at eighty-six was one of her "duchess trademarks." (Her nickname was Duchess.) Those of us who adored her, and we were legion, teased and enjoyed and admired her for this harmless vanity.

Virtue is not involved in this proverb, as far as I can see. But the heart is. As closely as any of us can come to holding up our part of a friendship with God, Mother did. Maybe back when the proverbs were written, people didn't dye their hair, but that's beside the point. Some of us allow our hair to go hoary, others don't. On the days when I know perfectly well that I'm *not* being friends with God, when even He can't "find me in the way of righteousness," my hoary head is certainly no crown of glory.

Especially is it no crown of glory on the days when I'm feeling a touch superior because I don't change its color and don't mind that the world knows I'm pushing seventy.

"He that is slow to anger is better than the mighty; and he that ruleth his spirit than he that taketh a city."

Proverbs 16:32

Read the daily newspapers and watch the TV news with this proverb beside you. The day on which I'm writing this happens to be one of worse than usual chaos in the world. Perhaps it isn't worse in God's eyes—men, women, and children have always met slowly painful and suddenly violent deaths every day in His world. And He knows about each one. Today, though, the news involves violence, angry response by my own country, so of course it is, to me, more depressing. The American-inflicted violence has been pronounced "a victory" by our government. Is it? Is any show of force in anger good in God's eyes?

Knowing human nature and the ugly potential of the human spirit out of control as God surely does, none of what's happening today surprises Him. He is never pulling for the Americans to "win," nor the French, nor the Jews, nor the Arabs, nor the British, nor the Cubans, nor the Soviets. He is pulling for us all to see the "better" way: to be slow to anger, to control our human spirits. "He that ruleth his spirit [is better] than he that taketh a city" or a small island or an entire nation.

Before I began to write here, I thought a long time about the young Man hanging on His Cross. That young Man *was* God. "I and the Father are one," He said. And "God *is* love." He is the only true definition of love any person will ever discover. There is no contradiction whatever between Jesus on His Cross and the God who said, "Come now, let us reason together."

Reason implies control of anger, the opposite of the human

spirit flailing about with heated rhetoric and rockets and missiles and tanks and bombs—killing and maiming to do what we call "win." What do we win? Certainly not the approval, the blessing of God. And even a moment's thought about the young Man on His cross shows painfully clearly that real might, real strength comes from what has been called Almighty weakness.

"The lot is cast into the lap; but the whole disposing thereof is of the Lord."

Proverbs 16:33

I am well aware that, in the main, women are historically against war. This does not cause me to blame men for allowing their human spirits to get out of control. Oh, God always knew our race would make war. Jesus reminded us that there would be "wars and rumors of wars." It can't be said too often that God is a realist. He has, from the beginning, watched us cast lots on the side of violent rebellion against some real or imagined tyranny and He has also watched us declare victory and defeat, then in a few years cast lots with violence again and start all over.

And He has heard both warring factions pray to Him for victory. Our leaders make speeches and our munitions factories make weapons and young and old men and women and children go on dying.

"The lot is cast into the [human] lap."

But, says the Lord, "I will ultimately decide it all."

"The whole disposing thereof is of the Lord."

He will one day be seen as the Victor and by His grace, our "laps" with all those futilely "cast lots" will be empty of every weapon but the one weapon He used from His cross—love.

"He that covereth a transgression seeketh love; but he that repeateth a matter separateth very friends."

Proverbs 17:9

This proverb is, as far as I can see, at least in part about gossip.

Gossip and its sad and often destructive consequences.

I'm sure I've written often (as have other writers) about the destructive consequences of plain old gossip. We have read and been told over and over that gossip is or can be character assassination. True. No one doubts that "repeating a matter separateth . . . friends." That it does is as self-evident as is the charge of character assassination.

But there is a deeper truth in this proverb, one I hadn't noticed until today.

"He that covereth a transgression seeketh love."

"Covering a transgression" simply means that we don't spout off about *everything* we know of a wrong inflicted. At times, it means "Just don't bring it up at all." But there is more: God says that if we remain silent under these conditions, then He *knows* that we are truly seeking *love.* Love is far different from the tempting thrill of shocking someone with a bit of sensational news. Love covers. Love protects. Love endures the boredom, often the dullness, of just keeping still.

"He that hath knowledge spareth his words: and a man of understanding is of an excellent spirit. Even a fool, when he holdeth his peace, is counted wise: and he that shutteth his lips is esteemed a man of understanding."

Proverbs 17:27-28

The writer of the proverbs seemed bent upon getting his point across here. Actually, the very first phrase, "He that hath knowledge spareth his words," says it all. But evidently this is important enough to follow the author's rule for emphasis: say it, then explain what you've just said and then give an illustration.

Here again, knowledge rightly applied equals understanding. To be a "man of understanding" seems to be the ultimate goal. *Not* to be a man who spews forth his great knowledge, but a man of *understanding.*

Even a fool, for the period of time in which he "holdeth his peace"—keeps his mouth shut—is wise.

Then the payoff line, simple and unmistakable: ". . . he that shutteth his lips is esteemed a man of understanding."

Do you ever sit in a room or at the other end of a telephone line and fidget while someone spouts on and on and on? Do you ever hear yourself spouting, stepping on the other person's comment, driving ahead to finish all you know about a subject?

I do a variety and a quantity of work in a day. I attempt, at least, to plan it each morning. Never do I remember to allow time for the telephone other than business calls. So when I get a call, I am usually the proverbial cat on a hot tin roof, no matter how much I like my caller. I answer the telephone at my desk and there I sit, surrounded with the work yet to be done. So, I mentally prowl about as I mean to be listening.

There's the rub. More often than not, quite unconsciously, I'm talking, talking in an effort to wind up the call. I'm human. What *I* have to say interests *me*. Rude. Thoughtless. (I'm not writing about gossip here.) What someone has asked, perhaps, is, "How's your novel going?" That's all the nudge I need. Talking about *my* interest is easy.

At those times, I am not showing one shred of *understanding* because "he [or she] that shutteth his lips is [the person] of [true] understanding."

Maybe that word "shutteth" will help. I am averse even to learning how anyone programs a computer, but perhaps now that I've put this down on paper, I can program my mind so that when the telephone rings, I will enter into a sincere exchange and then shutteth my lips.

"The spirit of man will sustain his infirmity; but a wounded spirit who can bear?"

Proverbs 18:14

Because I just used it, I still have the Revised Standard Version open beside me as I begin another day by reading yesterday's mail, noting it for a helper or answering myself. One letter struck me in particular: "Your little book *Getting Through the Night* saved my life. I want to follow my husband in death. My friends are overwhelming me with kindness and Scripture and haste. They keep saying I'm strong and it will be all right soon, when I'm desperately plowing through one moment at a time. You didn't push me in your book. You even wrote that people in grief just aren't able to think or read much. Thank you."

Whether the small book on handling grief kept this lady from suicide I have no way of knowing. I answered her, though, early today, and gave her this proverb, another I hadn't noticed before. There are no pat answers when one's spirit is wounded as hers is. Too much talking, even too much encouragement, at a time like that also shows lack of understanding. I simply reminded her that in her Bible sometime she could read for herself that God *understands* that the human spirit, when it is whole and healthy, can endure sickness. In this proverb, however, even God asks, "but a *wounded* spirit who can bear?"

He *is* understanding, and He can heal our pain, but He does not hurry us.

"Hast thou not known? hast thou not heard, that the everlasting God, the Lord, the Creator of the ends of the earth, fainteth not, neither is weary?"

Isaiah 40:28

I work every day except Sunday, no matter how I feel. Oh, a bad cold might stop me for a day or so and once I did experience the drama (it is!) and panic of vertigo through the writing of an entire novel. But most of us don't—can't—stop work just because we're moody or under the weather or tired. With ample reason over the years, I have known real exhaustion—when I am likely to misplace unanswered letters, even contracts—the kind of bone tiredness that doesn't stop with the bones, but seems to turn normally active brain cells to bone, too. Such exhaustion always comes for me at the end of a long promotion tour for a new book, not only because I seem to have a genius for saying Yes when I should have said No, but because I've been jerked out of my own normal life—silence and writing and reading—into an unfamiliar, almost mechanical race in cars on interstates or hours spent in airports, struggling to make my "writer's back" adapt to those cruel airport chairs. Smiling is good for anyone, but try it over a period of two months almost without pause.

I'm home writing these days, and so I'm not at all tired. But I will be again and maybe you are today. If so, here is an infallible help: *God doesn't get tired.*

"Hast thou not known? hast thou not heard, that the everlasting God, the Lord, the Creator of the ends of the earth, fainteth not, neither is weary?" But, you ask, "What good does that do me when I'm too weary to think straight?"

Well, isn't He the *focus* of our faith? We don't have faith in something inanimate, do we? Isn't our faith in the Person of the "everlasting God, the Lord, the Creator of the ends of the earth"?

"Yes," you argue, "but how does it help me that *He's* not tired?" I can only tell you how it helps me to be reminded that the Lord I follow is never weary. The very symptoms of my own weariness remind me that He is never distracted from my needs or the needs of the entire world because they exhaust Him, wear Him out. My body and my mind can be worn flat, but my spirit can be fresh in God because *He is fresh.* I can count on His strength when mine is gone. The strength that *"is* made perfect in weakness." His strength, my weakness.

Ready or not, it is another day and we need to get through it. We can, because the "everlasting God, the Lord, the Creator of the ends of the earth" lives in us.

And He never tires.

"Hast thou not known? hast thou not heard, that the everlasting God, the Lord, the Creator of the ends of the earth, fainteth not, neither is weary? [that] *there is no searching of his understanding.*"

Isaiah 40:28

I repeated the entire verse for your convenience here. If the first portion has become yours, now add the last line and you will experience an unfolding.

Not only are we assured that God never grows weary, we are also told that there is no point in trying to search for the limits to His *understanding* of our weariness, because there are no limits to be found.

The very worst kind of exhaustion is the kind that goes unnoticed by anyone. You may have worked hard all day for your family—most women with families do—and then, when the family comes home, they grab those clean shirts and blouses, gobble the labored-over meal, and go about their business. I'm told that generally no one says, "Gee, Mom," or "Gee, honey, you must have worked hard to get all this done. I'll bet you're tired." Wouldn't that help? Or you may be the member of your family whose responsibility it is to have enough money in the account to pay those bills. You come home worn to a nub and there are family plans for going out to dinner or having guests. Facing that busy evening after that busy day would be a lot easier, wouldn't it, if someone— anyone—said, "I'm sorry you're so tired. I know this has been a hard day."

Point made, I think. If no one around you notices your exhaustion, take heart. God notices *and* He understands.

"He giveth power to the faint; and to them that have no might he increaseth strength."

Isaiah 40:29

If knowing that God understands your exhaustion —physical or mental or spiritual—and that He pays attention are not enough, try this.

We have His word for it: "He giveth power to the faint." *He giveth.* How? How, when we've overworked, lost sleep because someone we love has just died or lies ill in a hospital, can He *give* strength? How is His "strength made perfect in weakness"?

I don't know.

No one knows.

No one except God, but He does. We dare not shun the *value* of mystery where our faith in Him is concerned. Most of us do, but we do it at our own risk. At the risk of missing His point altogether. Just because I don't know *how it is* that God can give me enough energy to get through the fourth TV interview in one day and the second four-hour autographing party—and still drive over a hundred miles that night—does not mean that He isn't going to give it to me. He has given enough strength to me hundreds of times. He has given it to millions and millions of us and He will go right on doing it because no one ever, ever slips God's mind.

The fact that we don't know how He does it is beside the point.

". . . they that wait upon the Lord shall renew their strength; they shall mount up with wings as eagles; they shall run, and not be weary; and they shall walk and not faint."

Isaiah 40:31

Read those lines again. The rhythm, the tempo, the energy of the words themselves seem to rise up. I am elevated by the movement of the very words themselves. I was intended to be elevated by those words.

You were intended to be elevated by them.

They are God's words to us for those weary, sodden times when absolutely nothing, no one short of "the everlasting God, the Lord, the Creator of the ends of the earth" can help.

All of us work better when we're fresh, not weary. There are those instances, though, when God seems bent on proving Himself to us, in spite of our exhaustion. Because of readers' and critics' positive reactions to my recent book *What Really Matters,* I am now convinced that there is a deeper meaning to these words than mere energy when we are fatigued. I wrote *What Really Matters* in a state of utter exhaustion after the deaths of my only brother and my mother *and* without missing a beat after the writing of my novel *Savannah,* a one-thousand-page manuscript. Contractually, I had to write *What Really Matters* when I did, and as I sat here day after day laboring away, I did not feel as though I was mounting up with wings of anything. Still, there seems to be a rush of His energy in its pages that far transcends me.

What did I do to be able to take that energy He promised? Nothing. That is, nothing spiritual-sounding or pious. I had no set-aside Bible study times, no prolonged or even definite prayer about it. I just sat down at the typewriter and thought in His Presence, "Lord, You *know* I'm too tired to write a book.

But You also know I have to do it or break a contractual agreement."

He did know my fatigue, He did know I had to do it. My only contribution, as I remember that numb period today, is that I kept at it until I was finished. I know also that a hundred times a day I stopped, blank as a wall, and had to sit here and wait. But I did wait. And I did keep a bookmark in place so that as often as necessary, I could open my Bible and read: ". . . they that wait upon the Lord shall renew their strength; they shall mount up with wings as eagles; they shall run, and not be weary; and they shall walk and not faint."

At times my "eagle wings" wouldn't have lifted a baby chicken, but the book got written because He knew my need and paid attention. Does sitting before a typewriter, dull of mind, blank of ideas, mean "waiting upon the Lord"? I guess it does if the exhausted writer *expects* His help.

Maybe all I did that was right was to be expectant. He makes us expectant if we give Him half a chance.

". . . behold, there was a man, whose appearance was like the appearance of brass, with a line of flax in his hand, and a measuring reed . . . so he measured the breadth of the building, one reed; and the height, one reed."

"I . . . looked, and behold a man with a measuring line in his hand. Then said I, Whither goest thou? And he said unto me, To measure Jerusalem, to see what is the breadth thereof, and what is the length thereof."

Ezekiel 40:3,5
Zechariah 2:1–2

What could those verses possibly have to do with the day ahead for you or for me? I leave it up to you to discover what might have meaning in your life. For me, aside from the oddly appealing prose, they have to do with God's personal concern with *form.* Painters, writers, dancers, sculptors, and musicians in particular should give thanks for that. But so should bakers of beautiful cakes and makers of dresses and designers of cars and architects of buildings and teachers of the young.

I awakened today in a state of uneasy confusion. I am at about the halfway point of the first draft of a new novel. So far, the form is a departure from my other novels because of the nature of the material in the opening chapters. Normally, a novel divides itself into three or four parts. This one does not. As of now, I can see only Part I and Part II and then The End. But the *form* of Part II is so vague and poorly defined to me right now, I wish I believed in so-called creative people throwing tantrums of temperament. I don't, so you are privy —firsthand—to what I try to do when confusion reigns. I opened my Bible and thought about what I might choose to write about in this book today. Late yesterday, I had rather planned to go to the New Testament. The confused *form* of Part II of the novel loomed like a thick, wholly shadowed wall. The truth was I could really concentrate on nothing else.

Why the "man with the measuring rod" in Ezekiel came to my struggling mind, I can't explain, except that I will never forget having read and marveled at the lyricism of Ezekiel the night of my own conversion to Christ more than thirty years ago. So, there I sat, hunting that lyrical part of the book of Ezekiel. And then, searching a concordance, I noticed a "man with a measuring line" in, of all places, Zechariah.

Out of this peculiar procedure have I found the right form for Part II of the novel? No. But the looming wall *is gone.* I will find it. Why am I so sure? Because I'm sure of God. And of His personal interest in all *form.* I am His child, so why would He keep me confused on the subject?

Look at any large or small part of His creation and see, as plainly as your hand before you, the creative extent of His involvement with *form:* any tree, plant, flower—the human hand. I can go on to the New Testament in this book now. When it's time, later on today, to tackle Part II of the novel, I count on knowing.

I count on the God of form.

New Testament

"Then Joseph being raised from sleep did as the angel of the Lord had bidden him, and took unto him his wife: And knew her not till she had brought forth her firstborn son: and he called his name JESUS."

St. Matthew 1:24–25 (read verses 18 through 25)

For the whole picture, I hope you will read verses 18 to 25. Everyone—even non-Christians—will find them familiar, but until today, I hadn't thought much about the extraordinary *balance* of Joseph. Christians are often thought odd because we believe that God is personally dependable. Some of us, let's face it, do seem odd, off-balance by the world's standards. But where is the *real* center of balance?

Think about Joseph for a minute. He had so many choices when, in his dream, the "angel of the Lord" told him to go right ahead and marry the young woman he loved even if she was going to have a baby—not by him. The human reaction to this would be to say "Forget it. If she doesn't love me enough to allow me to father her child . . ." The state of mind of a man who had allowed himself that understandably human reaction would be chaos. He would have had a good excuse to marry someone else, to become an alcoholic, to undergo an identity crisis, to wallow in self-pity. Joseph simply took God's word on the situation and not only married the young Mary, but "knew her not till she had brought forth her firstborn son." Joseph himself even named the Child Jesus as he had been told to do.

Who, by the standards of society, could be thought more peculiar or odd?

Follow Joseph's life throughout his years, though, and you will see an example of the true *balance* of the Holy.

"Now when Jesus was born in Bethlehem of Judaea in the days of Herod the king, behold, there came wise men from the east to Jerusalem, Saying, Where is he that is born King of the Jews? for we have seen his star in the east, and are come to worship him."

St. Matthew 2:1–2

Many people, even those with only a nominal Christian background, can recall those familiar lines from memory. They are a part of Christmas. In fact, like the Twenty-third Psalm and the Lord's Prayer, we've heard them so often we almost don't grasp what the lines say.

I awoke today feeling just plain dull. I knew I would work. I'm not ill. I'm not tired. Just dull. I'd much rather read my friend Madeleine L'Engle's superb new book *And It Was Good* than labor over one of my own. I'm my own boss. I could read Madeleine's book, but like most people, when it's a workday, I work. If anyone said to me today, "Your writing is so easy to read, it must just flow from inspiration," I wouldn't want to be responsible for what I might say in return. I am seldom inspired. I am simply a professional writer. And so I write.

Besides, look what I'm writing about here: a Baby, born in a manger who created—just by being born—such widespread interest that wise men made the long, long trip to find Him—to worship Him! I'm writing about the Baby who, by becoming one of us in circumstances and surroundings so lowly that the shabbiest person can identify with Him, caused His own star to shine forth from the heavens. *And I feel dull?*

Yes, but that's all right. Feelings are not my bedrock. He is.

And He not only brought out His own special star, "he *is* the bright and morning star." The God I follow can no more be dull than He can be weary. "He is my salvation," even from dullness.

"Agree with thine adversary quickly, whiles thou art in the way with him; lest at any time the adversary deliver thee to the judge, and the judge deliver thee to the officer, and thou be cast into prison."

St. Matthew 5:25

I don't think most of us give Jesus Christ much credit for having a true sense of humor.

Isn't He saying here that we'll all be a lot better off in our daily round if we don't keep digging the hole deeper for ourselves?

He did come to give us a more abundant life, as He said. I try to remember that He also meant a more abundant *daily* life. When someone pins me in a corner or when I've pinned someone else in a corner (say, a repairman who didn't really repair) I *try* to remember the wisdom behind what to me are these wise, humorous words of Jesus. Before either "adversary" gets carried away proving he or she is right, find a point of agreement, of understanding.

A lot of us dig the holes in which we find ourselves simply because we are too stubborn to "agree" quickly with anyone —least of all an adversary. I find humor in Jesus' literary exaggerations: He so wants peace for us that He took His analogy all the way from the adversary to the judge, to the officer, and finally to a jail cell!

Humor, but it also grabbed my attention.

"Ye have heard that it hath been said, An eye for an eye, and a tooth for a tooth: But I say unto you, That ye resist not evil: but whosoever shall smite thee on thy right cheek, turn to him the other also."

St. Matthew 5:38–39

I doubt that any two verses in the entire Bible have been so bypassed by humankind. Bypassed, ignored, even erased by you, by me, by our friends, by church members, by governments.

A headline in yesterday's newspaper read: U.S. PLANS RETALIATION IN LEBANON. RETALIATORY MILITARY ACTION IN OFFING.

Governments and people, while touting liberty and human rights, invade and *retaliate.*

I don't recall any use of either word by Jesus. To invade means to take. He said to *give.* Do you own two coats? Give one away.

Retaliate? He didn't actually use the word, but "an eye for an eye and a tooth for a tooth" defines retaliate. His response to retaliate is "turn to him the other [cheek] also."

Do we believe Him? We say we believe *in* Him. But do we believe Him? Few dare to voice it, but most of us appear to think, when forced to confront what He said here, "Resist not evil? That's crazy talk! Madness!"

Crazy talk from the Son of God? Madness?

Arm military troops called "peacekeepers" and stockpile weapons called "peacekeepers" in spite of what the Prince of Peace Himself said about *His* way of handling disputes?

We have to decide these things for ourselves, but I keep remembering that He also said "Follow me." He *didn't* say "Follow me in certain areas and not in others."

"And whosoever shall compel thee to go a mile, go with him twain. Give to him that asketh thee, and from him that would borrow of thee turn not thou away. Ye have heard that it hath been said, Thou shalt love thy neighbour, and hate thine enemy. But I say unto you, Love your enemies, bless them that curse you, do good to them that hate you, and pray for them which despitefully use you, and persecute you."

St. Matthew 5:41–44

Here it is again. More "madness." More "crazy talk." One of the strongest plots a novelist or playwright can use is the theme of revenge. It is that common to us all. It is natural with us to want to "get even." To "hate our enemies." To lock our doors when they appear. To let the telephone ring when they harass. To *show them* they can't "despitefully use you."

It is natural for humankind and for governments to stockpile weapons—both actual and symbolic. And I suppose it is also natural to skirt this statement of God's by calling that stockpile a "deterrent to war." That kind of twisted logic somehow gives us a vague aura of "peacemakers." It stretches my credulity to hear nuclear weapons called "peacekeepers," but in 1984 they're called that every day. I can't see this kind of rationalizing as anything but Madison Avenue sleight of hand. Some of God's people vote and pass pamphlets and expound on the need for arms and more arms. Jesus said, "Love your enemies, bless them that curse you, do good to them that hate you."

More mad, crazy talk from the Son of God, whom I call my Savior and Lord.

". . . when thou prayest, enter into thy closet, and when thou hast shut thy door, pray to thy Father which is in secret; and thy Father which seeth in secret shall reward thee openly. But when ye pray, use not vain repetitions, as the heathen do: for they think that they shall be heard for their much speaking."

St. Matthew 6:6–7

I am certainly not an authority on prayer. I simply pray. As you do. And none of what I write here is in any sense a criticism of any form of prayer that may give you a more definite sense that you are indeed talking to God.

As I have grown older, though, and as the friendship between the Lord and me has deepened, I've come to feel that perhaps my most meaningful prayer times are wordless. "Be not ye therefore like unto them [much speaking]," Jesus added, ". . . for your Father knoweth what things ye have need of, before ye ask him."

All I intend to say here is that, indeed, there is a true kind of wordless prayer—two friends, communicating inwardly. Even Jesus didn't seem to have had in mind a particular "prayer technique" that day when He spoke to His disciples about prayer. He gave them a model prayer, a prayer of intent: the Lord's Prayer, as we know it. So, words or no words —evidently, the intent is paramount.

Two friends can be together in the silence with genuine creativity in solace or joy or supplication. In my heart, I ask Him to do this or that. He also asks me.

"The light of the body is the eye: if therefore thine eye be single, thy whole body shall be full of light."

St. Matthew 6:22

I have spent an hour or so thinking about that familiar verse as written by St. Matthew and checking translations other than the King James. "If therefore thine eye be *single*" has clearer meaning for me. Other translations and paraphrases substitute words such as sound, unselfish, healthy, clear, and so on. All good, all add a dimension to what must be a key quotation from Jesus. He also told us that we, as Christians, as followers of His, are the "light of the world."

Are we? And what does it mean *being* light?

What, actually, does it mean to say that the "light of the body is the eye"? Some versions use "lamp" instead of "light." Fine.

"If therefore thine eye be *single*" brings to my mind the sharp, clear, single beam of the lantern I use when I need to go outside at night. The lantern's beam is sharp, focused, bright, *single.* It is not diffused. A bracket of burning candles or the mellow, dim lights on a Christmas tree may be prettier to look at, but that kind of soft light does not cut through to show clearly, to show *singly.*

My physical eyes are not "single" now as they were when I was young. Without my glasses, this minute, I can see only a blurring of black lines on the manuscript page as I write, but for the life of me I couldn't tell you what's there. My eye, my physical eye, is no longer single. No longer sound. No longer healthy.

Jesus always did His best to make His teachings clear. He used down-to-earth illustrations that we can understand by experiencing the things He talked about. But He seldom, if ever, had only one meaning. I fully believe He tried to make us think. This, of course, is why we can spend hours reading and rereading what He said, finding new dimensions, new light, new depths.

I feel, at least, that what I've seen in this familiar verse at the start of this day is more than I've seen before. The "more" has to do with the singleness, the healthiness, the soundness of my seeing. Not with my physical eye, of course, but with my inner, spiritual eye. It has to do with the clarity of the beam my light throws out upon events and circumstances and people around me.

Am I seeing with any degree of the clarity with which Christ sees? He offers us His sight—His single, sound, healthy, realistic sight of everything. Anxiety on our part blurs our vision and fractures our view of Him. When I am anxious, I am not full of light. If I am seeing clearly, singly, soundly, I am seeing Him as He is and I am able to reject anxiety because He is in charge.

"But if thine eyes be evil, thy whole body shall be full of darkness. If therefore the light that is within thee be darkness, how great is that darkness!"

St. Matthew 6:23

We stumble when it's dark, or we certainly tend to. I've used this illustration in other books, I'm sure, but since it's apt and since it happened to me again last night in my own familiar office, I'll repeat it. My friend and I were watching public television in her room, where the TV happens to be. The telephone rang. I hurried into my office at the opposite end of the house to answer. My office and bedroom form one fairly large space, divided only by folding doors that are seldom closed. Only a dim light burned by my bed. The telephone is on my desk at the other end of the room. At home, I never wear shoes, even in winter, so I cracked a bare toe on the leg of a table beside my desk as I sailed by. It was dark. I knew perfectly well that table was there. I hit it anyway.

This anecdote may sound obvious. It isn't. I had sense enough to turn on a light. I just didn't do it. I also knew that faulty vision—and darkness always brings faulty vision—can cause us to hurt ourselves even if we're in the most familiar territory.

When we look with an "evil" or unsound or unhealthy or unrealistic eye at any thing or any circumstance or any person, what we "see" is distorted by darkness. If we look again at the same thing or circumstance or person with God's eye, we find out "how great is that darkness!"

Now and then we read about or meet or see on television some person or group of persons who strike us as being just plain evil. Mean, hopeless, so evil we can only shake our heads or click our tongues and marvel that a human being could perform such totally dark, vile deeds. God, thank goodness, does not see anyone with that *lack* of light. If He did, we'd all be sunk.

God, in Jesus Christ, never looks at us with a diseased, unhealthy, unsound, blurred eye. Even in the dark. "Darkness and light are the same" to Him.

The Bible, if you notice, does not contain many exclamation marks. When I find one, I pay attention. There is one here: "If therefore the light that is within thee be darkness, how great is that darkness!"

Jesus said of Himself: "I am the light of the world." How great is our darkness without Him!

"No man can serve two masters: for either he will hate the one, and love the other; or else he will hold to the one, and despise the other. Ye cannot serve God and mammon. Therefore I say unto you, Take no thought for your life, what ye shall eat, or what ye shall drink; nor yet for your body, what ye shall put on. Is not the life more than meat, and the body than raiment?"

St. Matthew 6:24–25

All sorts of religious prejudices and practices have sprung from this passage. Of course the body is more than raiment, but does that mean we aren't to look our best? Does realizing that life is more than meat mean we are not to eat meat? Does the admonition that we cannot serve God and mammon mean that we are not to try to make money enough to dispatch our responsibilities and help others who might have less?

All those questions are extraneous to what Jesus is really saying. Always, He speaks of the kingdom of the inner life, not the material life of society. It took His disciples a long, long time to catch on to this fact, but it is essential. Serving God and mammon is not possible in the life of the spirit within. Serving mammon—*living* to get more and more money—is a full-time occupation and leaves no inner or outer space for the pursuit of God Himself. That is simple fact. In the plainest of language, He is saying that it is impossible to worship material possessions *and* God at the same time. But it doesn't necessarily mean He is urging us to take a vow of poverty.

To me, the goal of the Christian life is to bless God's reputation in the world by living *balanced,* sane lives: lives centered

115

in love, with possessions and personal appearance (raiment) and meat (food) in their proper places around that center.

If greed and the pursuit of money are central, we neglect the fruits of the spirit, no matter how often we declare that it is God who prospers us!

My beloved late friend Dr. E. Stanley Jones used to say, "A Christian should make all the money he can without disobeying God and then give away more than any so-called sensible financier tells him to give." I agreed with Brother Stanley thirty years ago when I first heard him say that. I agree today.

As I understand this passage, Jesus isn't saying "Don't serve God and mammon." He's saying "You can't do it." It just isn't possible.

". . . seek ye first the kingdom of God, and his righteousness; and all these things shall be added unto you."

St. Matthew 6:33

One of the many reasons why I am enjoying writing this little book is that more than ever before I now feel free to express my lingering questions with no guilt for not being able to come up with answers.

God does not mind our questioning.

I think He welcomes it.

I don't understand everything Jesus said and I doubt that you do. The longer I live, the more deeply and honestly I allow myself to think in God's presence, the less I seem to know about this verse. Oh, I'm sure I've written on it before. I know a zillion other authors have, some settling for the simplistic view that *if* we are "good Christians" God will reward us by giving us food and clothing and so on and on.

"Seek ye first the kingdom of God." That phrase always brings to mind a beautiful lady whose heart has for over fifty years sought first and only the kingdom of God and who is one of the poorest people I know by material standards. She has worked all her life, as has her husband, and what they have managed is not to starve. They had no house until they were given one by friends. She has ministered to those even less fortunate without ceasing. I had very, very little when I first met this loving lady, but I remember her gratitude when I managed to share two dollars with her once. I can also clearly remember the good ring of laughter when she told me, "'I couldn't afford cake ingredients, so I took the grieving family a pan of cornbread."

My truly Christian friend is no better off financially now than all those years ago and yet, she, above almost anyone I know, seeks "first the kingdom of God, and his righteousness." What's more she *finds* them both.

I write these pages early in 1984, when the American economy is suddenly supposed to look bright and booming. One of my longtime friends was married to a man who at his death was among the more than ten million still without jobs in the country. Together, they stood in church food lines about twice a week because their money ran out. His unemployment compensation was long gone and so was their home and car. They lived with her sister, and some of us remember to send a check now and then.

At Christmas, I received a note from her written on the back of a greeting card she had received last year. This is what the note said: "I am learning what Jesus meant when He said 'all these things shall be added unto you.'"

I knew that her husband, no longer able to face what he felt was his failure to provide for her, had killed himself just before Thanksgiving. For days, I had tried to find her new address to calm my own heart by offering some help. The only other message she wrote was this: "I am not giving you my new address since I know you have more letters than you can manage anyway, but I love you and God loves us all."

With all my heart, I hope she reads this and sends me that address. You can see she's depending upon Him and not upon me, or anyone else, to see that "all these things shall be added unto" her. I need her help far more than she needs mine.

I'd give almost anything to know what she's learned about trusting Him for her needs in these most heartbreaking circumstances.

It's no secret that today the rich do seem to get richer and the poor get poorer. God does not change society's policy, political or otherwise, so He must have something far deeper to say here than most of us realize.

". . . for your heavenly father knoweth that ye have need of all these things."

St. Matthew 6:32

Do we have need of a home, food, clothing, joy, security, medical care, work to do, a place to be and to belong?

Yes. Then does the Heavenly Father love so much less those who lack these things? Does He keep His promises only to those who succeed and never fall on bad times?

Could it be that again Jesus isn't even speaking of material needs but the kingdom within? The inner life of us all? Is He again speaking His singular truths in metaphors that we *should* be able to understand? And often don't?

I confess I'm not absolutely sure. In the novel I'm writing, part of the action takes place in what was once the Cherokee Nation in northern Georgia. Unlike some more warlike Indian tribes and nations (and I certainly understand why they felt warlike toward the white settlers), the Cherokees took what they believed to be a higher road. Moravian missionaries in the old Cherokee Nation had converted many Cherokees to Christianity. As in all Christian groups, with some of the converted Indians the Christianity "took" and with others it didn't.

In the year 1832, a few Cherokee leaders, thinking it safer for their own skins, signed a treaty with the U.S. government and were promptly sent away from their beloved northern Georgia mountains to the West. Many of them were Christians. The majority stayed behind—not fighting with guns and arrows, but peaceably, through the U.S. courts, struggling to keep the lands they so loved and revered. Lands that, of course, were coveted by white people. Now perhaps the first group of Christian Cherokees, who left while the leaving was easier, made the better human judgment. That is really beside the point. The second group, under their truly Christian chief, John Ross, stayed, tried to reason with our far less cultured government leaders in Georgia and Washington, and lost. At government bayonet point, men, women, and children were prodded into stockades, penned up, and forced to march over what is now called the Trail of Tears to far beyond the Mississippi.

Didn't God care about these peace-loving Cherokee children of His?

Why, when they even went so far as to pattern their own government after that of the United States, when they prayed night and day, negotiated by Christian reason, were not their beloved lands "added unto them"? Did God turn a deaf ear to their prayers? Didn't he know "that they had need of these things"?

He knew. The only explanation I can give is that along that weary, heart- and spirit-breaking march west, away from the mountains they had loved for so long, one of them was able to pray, "We know You walk and weep *with us*, Jesus Christ."

Jesus said so much in each word of this portion of St. Matthew's Gospel that none of us is likely ever to plumb the depths of it.

What I can see at this point in my own pilgrimage is that most of the time we don't think on His level or share His values. I see that and have to keep remembering that whether we understand or not, *He is in charge.*

Is the knowledge that He is with us more essential than being warm, fed, protected? What a hard question if we truly seek kingdom values. Nowhere in any of these promises of Jesus is there a hint that luxury is to be bestowed upon us, no matter how diligently we seek the kingdom first. But those of us who do have access to plenty make fools of ourselves if we begin to feel at all special because God "is prospering us." Beware here. Beware also of feeling no responsibility for those who suffer from want of any material kind.

A close friend cannot afford her suddenly elevated heating bills and so she hurries, shivering, to her kitchen to put together a meal and flies back to her bedroom to eat it because that is the only room in her house she can afford to heat. For me to pray for her is far from enough. How do I know that I am not a means of God's adding "all these things unto her"?

"Take therefore no thought for the morrow: for the morrow shall take thought for the things of itself. Sufficient unto the day is the evil thereof."

St. Matthew 6:34

❧ ❧ ❧

Here, the creative mind of Jesus is attempting again to make us think.

"Take . . . no thought for the morrow."

The RSV reads: "Therefore do not be anxious about tomorrow."

Even preferring the rhythms of the King James, I have to admit that substituting the word "anxious" for "thought" helps. It is human nature—very human nature—to worry, to be anxious about what tomorrow holds or could hold. No one understands human nature or the needs of human nature as clearly as God understands them. On His Cross, Jesus went as far as even God could go because He *did* understand the needs and anxieties of our earthbound natures.

I am grateful every day of my life that He bothered to give this specific warning about the danger of adding tomorrow's anxieties to those of today. Sometimes I wish I earned my living at work planned for me and expected of me by someone else instead of by me alone. First of all, I take on the responsibility of agreeing to a submission date for a manuscript when the contract is signed. Then, once I come up with a book idea, I lay out my own work schedule and over the long months hold myself to it. I am a tough boss. Do I ever grow anxious that the person whom I boss will fail? Is spinach green? And so, particularly on the days when I am feeling dull or slow, I seem to have reason for double anxiety. Not only do I get both frightened and anxious that the person whom I boss won't be up to the task, I have the boss's anxieties too that the contract won't be met.

Writers are far from alone in all this.

A young mother once told me that she, too, carries double anxiety at times. After all, a part of her own nature, personality, heritage, and body are in that child who will pass or fail in school, and so she is anxious for them both.

But isn't it like our Lord to have anticipated all our anxieties for whatever reasons? And wasn't He tender and sensitive and thoughtful to be so specific about them?

I wonder why it is that when anxiety is such a heavy burden we go right on reaching for tomorrow's load today. Most of us do. I am sincerely trying, though, and with some success these days, to form the habit of remembering that it was the God of the universe who said you only have to live one day at a time.

"Therefore whosoever heareth these sayings of mine, and doeth them, I will liken him unto a wise man, which built his house upon a rock: And the rain descended, and the floods came, and the winds blew, and beat upon that house; and it fell not: for it was founded upon a rock."

St. Matthew 7:24–25

In the next verse, Jesus is equally as graphic in describing the consequence of having built a house upon sand. (I hope you will take time to read all that precedes these verses in Chapter 7.) He spoke to the people that day in Palestine, a mountainous country where quick storms blow up and not only flood creek beds that were dry minutes before but sweep away all sandy mounds or knolls. As always, He was careful to use illustrations familiar to His listeners. Palestinian people understood exactly what He meant. But living on a flat coastal island within three miles of the Atlantic Ocean, I understand too. As do those who live in any part of a land where torrents of rain fall, or below towering mountains where heavy snows melt.

In recent years, our coastlines have been turned into places of potential destruction and even death. Hurricanes are not uncommon here, and with the once protective sand dunes bulldozed away to make room for still more houses, nothing but those houses, flimsy at best when a hurricane strikes, are there to "protect" the more inland homes.

You get the point, I'm sure. The warning of Jesus did not apply only to Palestine. We are all told to build our houses upon "rock" if we are to be eternally secure. And, of course, He was again illustrating with an earthy example, a spiritual truth.

Most important, it seemed to me as I reread this chapter today, is His total claim to *be* God, to speak in such an authoritative way that no one could mistake the fact that His words applied irrevocably to the eternal world of the spirit. Oh, He pronounced His identity more pointedly when He told His disciples outright that "I and the Father are one," but it is here, too. "I and the Father are *one.*" The Rock. The one Rock on which it is safe to entrust our eternal lives.

Either He was telling the truth or He wasn't.

That is for us to decide. "For he taught them as one having *authority,* and not as the scribes."

"And when Jesus was entered into Capernaum, there came unto him a centurion, beseeching him, And saying, Lord, my servant lieth at home sick of the palsy, grievously tormented. And Jesus saith unto him, I will come and heal him. The centurion answered and said, Lord, I am not worthy that thou shouldest come under my roof: but speak the word only, and my servant shall be healed."

St. Matthew 8:5–8

The centurion then explained to the Master that he quite understood the power of real *authority*. The man was an officer in the army. When he gave a command it was obeyed because of his authority. He had servants. When he gave them an order, it was also obeyed.

I like to imagine the look on Jesus' face at that moment. His own personal fulfillment must have been overwhelming! We are told that "he marveled." I'm sure the Lord didn't toss off a quick answer to this trusting man. I can imagine that He gave the centurion a long, penetrating, probably delighted look, then was silent for a time. In a moment, He said to those standing about in the crowd who had overheard the conversation, "Verily I say unto you, I have not found so great faith, no, not in Israel."

This centurion was not an Israelite. He was a Gentile. He had not been taught Hebrew law. But, perhaps weary of the signs around him in the pagan world in which he lived, the man was strangely attracted to Jesus, saw in Him the very authority of God . . . and displayed far deeper insight into true spiritual reality than Jesus had found even in Israel.

In a way, I feel real identity with this centurion. At the

moment I recognized Jesus of Nazareth as God incarnate, I began to believe with my whole heart that He could do anything! And like the centurion, I didn't know one book in the Bible from another.

"And Jesus said unto the centurion, Go thy way; and as thou hast believed, so be it done unto thee. And his servant was healed in the selfsame hour."

St. Matthew 8:13

When someone asks me if I believe in healing, I tell them that I believe that all things are possible with God. Actual physical healing is an area in which I still have as many questions as you may have.

I once prayed for the healing of a friend with a congenital limp. He was healed. I saw it with my own eyes. That prayer took place many years ago. My friend still does not limp. Thank God, though, the happy event did not cause me to decide suddenly that I had any special powers of healing or that I should go around for the remainder of my life as a "healer." I say thank God because I'd be sunk if I allowed anything but Christ Himself—even something as much a part of Him as healing—to lodge in the center of my life. From the very first year of my walk with Him, I have been convinced that Christians who make the Bible, baptism, healing, witnessing, the church, or communion *central* will likely slip off balance. He said, "I if I be lifted up will draw all men unto me." We dare allow nothing but Jesus Himself to be our center.

To me, the important line in St. Matthew 8:13 is "as thou hast *believed*, so be it done unto thee." It certainly seems that God does not heal everyone who asks or is prayed for. He does heal many—some directly, others by medical treatment. But what if we *believed*—put down our eternal weights—on healing itself?

Some of you, after reading this, may tell a friend, "Eugenia

Price does not believe in healing." Some of you may write to me and try to enlighten me.

The truth is, I believe that Jesus Christ can heal any human distortion. But I'll go right on actually *believing*, depending only on the Savior Himself. If I really trust Him, whatever He *does* will somehow be all right. I don't necessarily think He was trying to "preach healing" with the centurion that day. Healing happened to be the nature of the centurion's request. Jesus put His emphasis on the *quality* of the man's faith. The quality and the scope of it—"I have not found *so great* faith, no, not in Israel."

The nature of the request happened to be the healing of a sick servant. No one could or can see into the centurion's heart but Jesus, and what He saw there was total recognition of *who* the Healer was. The officer recognized the sole Authority over eternal wholeness.

"Come unto me, all ye that labour and are heavy laden, and I will give you rest. Take my yoke upon you, and learn of me; for I am meek and lowly in heart: and ye shall find rest unto your souls."

St. Matthew 11:28–29

❧ ❧ ❧

Can anything new be written about this well-loved, familiar passage from St. Matthew's Gospel?

Yokes are not burdensome things—yokes are helpful. Two walking in a yoke distribute the burden, lighten it. The words "labour" and "heavy laden" have been explained and elaborated upon as anything tiring, difficult, weakening, cumbersome, life-negating. We have been told that Jesus is "meek and lowly in heart" and of course a lot of us have misunderstood both "meek" and "lowly," so that Jesus has been erroneously depicted as being a mollycoddle, weak, submissive. That's nonsense, of course. "Lowly" means humble, not self-effacing. And there *is* no power on earth to match the "Almighty meekness" of the powerful young Man hanging on His Cross. The phrase "rest unto your souls" is clear. It must mean we can stop agitating, being anxious, worrying, fretting.

I'm not going to say that I haven't written what I am about to write before because I have—again and again. But each time I've written or spoken of it or reread this one phrase, I have myself been given new insight into what it *can* mean to us. The phrase I speak of is the one least thought about in the entire passage: "learn of me."

The newer translations almost always diminish the power of this King James phrase for me. They say "Learn *from* me." Well, surely, He was—is—the world's greatest teacher. Still, I cling for my own unfolding insight into the power-packed short phrase "learn *of* me."

"Discover me."

It is as though Christ were saying, "Find out for yourself—firsthand—what I'm really like," *and then* you won't hesitate for a minute to "come unto me," to believe that "I will give you rest." You won't hesitate "to take my yoke upon you," to discover the exact meaning, the power-packed reason for my lowly humility.

"Learn of me" and you will have no reason *not* to follow me. "Learn of me" and the more you discover my true nature, the greater will be your own faith. We trust a person only if we know that person.

"Learn of me." And rest.

"At that time Jesus went on the sabbath day through the corn; and his disciples were an hungred, and began to pluck the ears of corn, and to eat. But when the Pharisees saw it, they said unto him, Behold, *thy disciples* do that which is not lawful to do upon the sabbath day. But he said unto them, Have ye not read what *David did, when he was an hungred,* and they that were with him; How he entered into the house of God, and did eat the shewbread, which was not lawful for him to eat, neither for them which were with him, but only for the priests?"

St. Matthew 12:1–4

You may think I have italicized some rather peculiar phrases in this passage. But I did it because I've seen something I haven't noticed before. The critical Pharisees were careful not to accuse Jesus of disobeying the sabbath laws by picking corn *Himself,* so they accused only His disciples. This makes me smile. And so does His response: "Have ye not read what David did, when he was an hungred, and they that were with him; How he entered into the house of God, and did eat the shewbread, which was not lawful for *him* to eat.?" David's men were with him that day as were Jesus' disciples. By including David, Jesus left no doubt in anyone's mind but that He, too, was hungry and picked some corn because of it!

There is no doubt in my mind, either, that the Pharisees, even in their annoyance and irritation with Jesus for "breaking the law," stopped short of accusing Him directly for a reason. He was turning their legalities upside down, so that they plagued and harassed Him for what appeared to their rigid minds to be blasphemy against the Lord God—still they rather feared Him. At least, they didn't quite dare accuse Him face to face.

Jesus stood right up to them, of course, in His use of the David analogy. He also further developed His response: "Or have ye not read in the law, how that on the sabbath days the priests in the temple [the Pharisees' priests in the Pharisees' own temple!] profane the sabbath, and are blameless?" And then He let the real explosion of truth happen: "I say unto you that in this place [undoubtedly pointing to Himself] is one greater than the temple."

I can't despise the Pharisees—if I did, I'd be as legalistic as they—because according to their old laws and in their darkness about the real identity of this carpenter from Nazareth who made such explosive remarks, He was shocking beyond words.

"A greater one than the temple is here."

The very Body of Christ was there! Not only in Jesus Himself, but in His disciples. The Body of Christ was there claiming to be greater than the Pharisees' holy temple itself.

My beloved friend Dr. Anna B. Mow has thrown a beam of bright light on this very question for me, which I cannot forget because I keep learning from it: "Genie, remember, the Body of Christ and the organized church are *not* necessarily one and the same. They can be, but they sometimes are not."

"But I say unto you, That in this place is one greater than the temple . . . if ye had known what this meaneth, I will have mercy, and not sacrifice, ye would not have condemned the guiltless. For the Son of man is Lord even of the sabbath day."

St. Matthew 12:6–8

Even while He was pointedly exposing the spiritual darkness of the highly religious Pharisees who were again trying to trick Him, Jesus was also showing the same quality of forgiveness and mercy He would soon show from the Cross. "If ye had *known* what this meaneth, I will have mercy, and not sacrifice, ye would not have condemned the guiltless."

From the Cross, He prayed, "Father, forgive them, for they *know not* what they do."

Those of us who follow this Lord of mercy and forgiveness dare not allow the roots of despising to grow in us. Peter vowed that no one loved Jesus as much as he loved him—just before denying Him. We are not showing love for Jesus if—simply because we happen to see His meaning where legality is concerned—we despise those who do not see it.

I seem to have to learn this lesson again and again. Doctrine-bound legalistic Christians are very, very hard for me to love. I have great difficulty keeping my mouth shut when a professed Christian argues in favor of the death penalty. To me, the death penalty is *pre*-Christian. "Ye have been taught an eye for an eye, but I say unto . . . ," Jesus said. I am as horrified as anyone at the thought of one human being murdering another, but I do not see that murdering the murderer improves anything.

"If ye had known what this meaneth, I will have *mercy,* not sacrifice."

Well, I need to have mercy toward those who call me a bleeding heart.

Back in the eighteenth and nineteenth centuries, self-respecting parents severely flogged their healthy, active youngsters for sneaking out to play tag on the sabbath. Doctors say it is a sacrifice—a painful one—for children with growing muscles to sit still for any length of time. "I will have mercy, not sacrifice."

True mercy implies compassion that forbears punishment even when justice demands punishment. Punishment involves sacrifice for the punished. The forgiveness of the God of the Cross is beyond human capacity for mercy. It is human to declare, "He or she did this evil thing, let there be like punishment."

There is nothing in God's forgiveness that implies getting even. We had *all* better give thanks that God's mercy is great enough to be *beyond* our understanding.

"And Jesus came and spake unto them, saying, All power is given unto me in heaven and in earth . . . and, lo, I am with you alway, even unto the end of the world."

St. Matthew 28:18, 20

Almost from the moment of my first encounter with Jesus Christ, now more than thirty years ago, I have believed that—in good times and troubled times—He is with me. I don't necessarily *feel* His presence. Pressures and problems can distract me as they distract you, but my feelings don't count. What counts is that we can believe Him and He said that He would never leave us.

"Lo, I am with you alway, even unto the end of the world." Either He meant it or He didn't.

I am eternally convinced that there is no way by which I can ever be away from Him, because He will never be away from me. Oh, you and I can put up barriers of disobedience, self-pity, arrogance, and so on, but the barriers are on our side. Never on His.

In various forms, I have written of this before. Not only does it bear repeating and repeating, I want to add a new confirmation that should give still more courage. It takes courage to go right ahead *acting* as though we feel His Presence when we don't. This is the confirmation: *before* He assured His disciples that He would be with them always, He took the time to be specific about His nature: "All power is given unto me in heaven and in earth." *All power.*

His earthly ministry—even from the Cross and the open tomb—was behind Him when He told them that. He could and did speak with a new power, saying in effect, "Not only am I with you always, but my Presence means that you have ready access to all power in heaven and in earth."

137

Think of that!

It helps to have shared the same trouble or heartache when we try to give comfort to another person, but because of what Jesus said, it isn't necessary. It so happens that I've never had an operation of any kind except a tonsillectomy when I was two or three, and I don't remember it. I can't say to a friend about to enter the hospital that I know from experience that He will be there every minute too. But I can say it with total confidence because He said He would be.

Of course, I can witness to His unwavering, steady Presence in other trying times—the pressures of work, financial panic, the heavy moments spent beside still open graves of loved ones. What matters, though, is that He did not in any way *qualify* that promise! He did not say "I will never leave you" if you are good or faithful or in this or that need. He simply said "I am with you always." Not "I will be," not "maybe." He said I am already with you and since "all power is given unto me in heaven and in earth," nothing, *nothing* can separate us.

"And there arose a great storm of wind, and the waves beat into the ship, so that it was now full. And he [Jesus] was in the hinder part of the ship, asleep on a pillow: and they awake him, and say unto him, Master, carest thou not that we perish? And he arose, and rebuked the wind, and said unto the sea, Peace, be still. And the wind ceased, and there was a great calm. And he said unto them, Why are ye so fearful? how is it that ye have no faith? And they feared exceedingly, and said one to another, What manner of man is this, that even the wind and the sea obey him?"

St. Mark 4:37–41

Fairly often I receive letters from readers—usually pages long—in which they explain their lack of spiritual growth, their puny faith, their sense of being far from God. Always, they mention that they are guilty over these feelings. "My wife has been dead for more than five years and I don't feel as close to God as the day of her funeral. I know the Lord keeps His promises, so it must be my fault."

Well, if it can be called a fault for being human, then I suppose it is our fault. Though, in such turmoil, guilt can be beside the point. No one can do professional counseling by mail, but it can be suggested in a letter that professional counseling be sought. To this depressed gentleman, I wrote: "See your minister or a Christian counselor you can trust and ask him or her about the disciples in the boat with Jesus the day He calmed the storm. I happen to believe that we can block our own liberation from a lot of troubles by *refusing to accept our own humanity.* Think for a minute about those disciples—right in the same boat with their Master—evidently with enough faith to ask Him to help, but after He did calm the wind and

139

the sea, they still 'feared exceedingly.' More than that, after having lived with Him day in and day out and after having heard His public and private teaching, they showed no concrete evidence of realizing who He really was!"

Then I asked, "Sir, are you not missing the point of all this? We now know that the Man-God, Jesus, was, is *one* with the Father. We no longer need to ask 'What manner of man is this?' All power in heaven and in earth has been given to Him —He is God's revelation of Himself. Ask your counselor if it is possible that you might still be as much in the dark—the humanly understandable dark—as the men in that boat. Maybe you need to let go of your guilt for giving your human attention to the storm that still buffets you, and by your will put your attention on the real identity of the One who can control all our seas and winds."

"And he went out from thence, and came into his own country . . . and when the sabbath day was come, he began to teach in the synagogue: and many hearing him were astonished, saying, From whence hath this man these things? . . . Is not this the carpenter, the son of Mary, the brother of James, and Joses, and of Judah, and Simon? and are not his sisters here with us? And they were offended at him. But Jesus said unto them, A prophet is not without honour, but in his own country, and among his own kin and in his own house. And he could there do no mighty work, save that he laid his hands upon a few sick folk, and healed them."

St. Mark 6:1–5

Mark's brief, swift account of Jesus' near failure in His own hometown leaves little more to be added. (I go on marveling that Mark could say so much in such few words!) One thing has struck me today, though: here is a quick, pointed explanation of why some of God's work seems rather futile.

Some of God's work futile?

Superficially, that's what Mark's account sounds like: "he could do there no mighty work, save that he laid his hands upon a few sick folk, and healed them."

I don't pretend to understand much about why prayer sometimes is answered and why at times it seems not to be. Mark gives one explanation. To those "few sick folk" who took Jesus seriously that day in His hometown came healing. The Master's hands had not lost their power. He had not. The problem, it seems to me, lay in the townsfolk themselves.

They heard the astounding things He said. They had also heard of His fame, but perhaps to boost their self-esteem they put Jesus down: "Oh, we knew him when he was growing up into a mere carpenter! He's just one of Mary's boys. Where does he get off saying such things and performing such acts? We're offended by this upstart."

Jesus' heart was not closed to them. Their hearts were closed to Him. Except for the "few sick folk," who evidently believed that *He was God,* not merely "one of Mary's boys."

Those few *were* healed that day. The others, it seems to me, could not be, because they went about minimizing the Healer. Undoubtedly many who were not healed asked to be, but in their hearts they were asking the favor of "Mary's boy," not the One who "in the beginning . . . was God." Not the One who that day stood before them in a familiar body—a young man they'd known since childhood—claiming authority equal with the Creator God. He so stunned the people in His hometown that they let His human familiarity blind them to His eternal identity.

The townsfolk of Nazareth weren't—aren't—alone in this. I grew up hearing about Jesus of Nazareth, yet at the moment thirty-three years later when I first began to see Him as God, I was the most astounded of all.

"And Jesus cried with a loud voice, and gave up the ghost. And the veil of the temple was rent in twain from the top to the bottom. And when the centurion, which stood over against him, saw that he so cried out, and gave up the ghost, he said, Truly this man was the Son of God."

St. Mark 15:37–39

❧ ❧ ❧

It has never bothered me that there appear to be contradictions, differing views of events in the four Gospels. As a writer, as a human observer, I know that no two persons see the same happening in exactly the same way. Matthew, for example, uses far more words than Mark.

Mark writes: "Jesus cried with a loud voice, and gave up the ghost. And the veil of the temple was rent." Matthew tells us also that there was an earthquake at that moment; that the rocks broke apart and that graves were opened and many bodies of the saints were seen to get up. Then Matthew recounts that *after* seeing all those happenings, the centurion declared Jesus to have been the Son of God.

I love both accounts. Today, it just happens that Mark's abbreviated account set me thinking. Mark didn't even mention that the centurion saw the veil of the temple being rent. He simply says, "When the centurion, which stood over against him, [was near Jesus on His cross] saw that he so cried out . . . he said, Truly this man was the Son of God."

How can we know at what moment, by what means, the Lord convinces a human heart, a human mind that He is, indeed, God?

Many, I suppose, prefer Matthew's more detailed account. He offers more *reasons* for the conversion of the centurion at that earthshaking moment when Jesus died. People tend to demand reasons. Poets, I think, don't. Mark is certainly a kind of poet.

Matthew, so strong on detail, as tax collectors and ex-tax collectors generally are, supplied several reasons for those who need them.

I tilt toward the mystery, the poetic inner motion of Mark's telling.

Either way is fine. And rather than disturbing me that there are differing accounts in these two Gospels, it reassures me that since He cares equally for all of us, this is, truly, God's word.

It tells me, too, that reasons, formulas, rituals, and set "plans of salvation" exist only to help *us*. God doesn't need them.

"And as he said these things unto them, the scribes and the Pharisees began to urge him vehemently, and to provoke him to speak of many things: Laying wait for him, and seeking to catch something out of his mouth, that they might accuse him."

St. Luke 11:53–54

I thought for a time about these verses today and shared a smile with the Lord. He does seem to have put Himself through just about all the temptations we can ever face.

Not often, I'm happy and grateful to say, but now and then my mailbox contains some concrete evidence that a few people out there are "laying wait," seeking to catch something out of my mouth.

Last week, in the same mail delivery there were two such letters. The first was from a gentleman who had read in a book of mine called *Diary of a Novel* that I admired President Jimmy Carter. As a consequence, he had jumped to the conclusion that I must be a wild-eyed liberal who approved of abortion, the nuclear freeze, did not want prayer in schools, and so on. My correspondent evidently had some distorted convictions about President Carter, and those convictions gave him the perfect excuse to accuse me.

The other letter, well written, sharply worded, obviously came from a highly educated lady, who loved and collected my historical novels for her own library—*until* she happened to read one of my inspirational titles. That did it. She now knows that since I am a Christian, I "must be one of those rigid, unloving, war-mongering, anti-ERA, environment-destroying 'conservatives.'"

Well, no one writes books for *everybody*.

I doubt that any man or any woman has ever been attacked as Jesus was, and any small identification with Him delights me.

"And they brought unto him also infants, that he would touch them: but when his disciples saw it, they rebuked them. But Jesus called them [his disciples] unto him, and said, Suffer little children to come unto me, and forbid them not: for *of such is the kingdom of God.* Verily I say unto you, Whosoever shall not receive the kingdom of God as a little child shall in no wise enter therein."

St. Luke 18:15–17

I'm sure the disciples meant well when they tried to protect Jesus from the confusion of parents bringing children. After all, they must have reasoned, the Master was already tired from throngs of adults. Children too would be just too much for Him.

Jesus did not lecture the parents—He lectured His own men. And I'm sure it must have been frustrating to Him to see that after all this time, after all His careful, personal, private teaching, the disciples still had not caught on to His real nature. For that matter, here they proved that neither had they seen the believer's real secret.

Now I'm sure some of these children were adorable, others —as is always true with children—not so adorable. Some were shy and timid, others noisy, crying perhaps, or climbing all over Jesus. He loved them all. But His meaning here goes far deeper than that. He intended to bless the children, to welcome them, but He also saw a fine opportunity to tell His followers—not strangers, His *followers*—that only trusting hearts can enter the kingdom of God.

After all, until children grow old enough for our cynicism

to infect them, they *trust.* Until someone proves untrustworthy, they simply take the word of that person and act on it.

"Verily I say unto you, Whosoever shall not receive the kingdom of God *as a little child* shall in no wise enter therein."

"And a certain ruler asked him, saying, Good Master, what shall I do to inherit eternal life? And Jesus said unto him, Why callest thou me good? none is good, save one, that is, God."

St. Luke 18:18–19

꙳꙳ ꙳꙳ ꙳꙳

Most of you know the remainder of this story told by Luke and Matthew. In the Gospel of St. Matthew, the ruler is called a young ruler. And as the conversation between him and Jesus moves along, we learn that the ruler is certainly respectable; he knows the Ten Commandments and honors them. The problem arises when Jesus, seeing that the young man's riches are at the center of his life, tells him he'll have to sell everything, give it to the poor, and follow Him to obtain eternal life.

Many penetrating sermons have been preached on that point. Today, in reading the entire story in St. Luke 18:18–25, I saw something I hadn't seen before.

My attention was caught, in fact, early in the narrative, at verse 19. Again, Jesus is responding to a question with a question: "Why callest thou me good? none is good, save one, that is, God."

A dear friend of mine who tries often to argue with me that Jesus of Nazareth was undoubtedly the world's greatest teacher *and* human being, but that He was *not* God Himself visiting the earth among us, invariably uses this verse as his "proof text." To my friend, Jesus is Himself admitting that He is merely a highly spiritual man. "Why callest thou me good? None is good, save one, that is, God."

"Proof texts" can be manipulated. I believe quite simply that Jesus was all that could be contained of God Himself in a being both divine and human. I know of no other way of

149

finding out anything definite about the nature of God. And just minutes ago, I found myself wondering if this rather abrupt question of Jesus' isn't His way—considering the young ruler's obvious education and intelligence—of asking him point blank if he believes Jesus really came from God?

In other words, was Jesus asking, "Why call me good Master? Do you call me that because you know that there is only one who is truly good and that One is God Himself? And that *I and the Father are one?"*

[Read St. Luke 24:1–7] "And they remembered his words, And returned from the sepulchre, and told all these things unto the eleven, and to all the rest. It was Mary Magdalene, and Joanna, and Mary the mother of James, and other women that were with them, which told these things unto the apostles. And their words seemed to them [the apostles] as idle tales, and they believed them not."

St. Luke 24:8–11

Have you ever wondered why the *women* believed in the resurrection *before* the men who had actually followed Jesus for three years? No, this is not going to be a feminist diatribe, nor a defense of the spiritual sensitivity of women over men.

I believe it is a legitimate question.

A revered Bible scholar once declared (I heard him!) that the women believed first because women were so ignorant in those days. Some of us in his audience—women and men—smiled at the dogma of the elderly preacher. I honestly don't know of any place in the New Testament where Jesus declares that *ignorance* leads to believing. Rather, He said that *child-likeness* makes it possible to enter the kingdom of heaven.

Perhaps there really *is* no specific answer to the question I've raised, only some possible theories. Women spent more time (as is sometimes still true) in the company of children. Perhaps these women learned from children what the Master meant when He laid down that one condition for entering the kingdom. Or perhaps, being diminished by a male-dominated society, women were quicker to see their own need. We all tend to believe what we *need* to believe. The more plainly I see my need, the stronger can grow my faith.

I can hear a female voice reminding me, "At least it's obvious why the men didn't *believe* the women when they told them Jesus had risen as He said. The men were sure they knew better. They were in the inner circle. Women have wild imaginations and talk too much, etc., etc."

I won't get into debate, but I have my own opinions as you have yours. I feel comfortable, at least, thinking that these women—Mary Magdalene, in particular—had heightened sensitivity because of heightened need.

"In the beginning was the Word, and the Word was with God, and the *Word was God.*"

St. John 1:1

I have written before on that verse. Many times. The reason is that, to me, this is the most important verse in the entire Bible. To me, it has always been and will always be. I became a believer, not because of that verse exactly, but because of what it says. In retrospect, it now seems that in an instant after the friend who led me to Christ assured me that to her God *was* Jesus Christ, I began to believe, to *know,* that for anyone the Lord of the universe, the Mighty God, *is knowable.* Jesus is not only, as my friend Helen Shoemaker wrote, "God's explanation for everything," *He is God,* or this verse is false.

John, perhaps closest in a personal way to Jesus when He was on earth, left no doubt. Either you believe what John wrote or you don't.

"In the beginning was the Word, and the Word was with God, and the Word *was* God."

In the King James version, the sentence is perfectly formed, filled with poetry, music, the true simplicity of all great art. But that, in itself, would not be enough, even for those who love superb writing. As though to help us understand that what this sentence declares *is* key to all true understanding of Christianity—of God Himself—John took pains, as he wrote on, to make it still clearer. We will think about that clarification on the following pages.

For now, for your own sake, for the sake of those whose lives touch yours, read and reread John 1:1 and allow it to become part of you. If, by faith, you believe this one sentence, your confusion about God's character, His attitudes toward us, His intentions, *has to vanish.*

"In the beginning was the Word, and the Word was with God, and the Word was God."

Let it become as much a part of you as breathing.

"The same was in the beginning with God. All things were made by him; and without him was not any thing made that was made."

St. John 1:2–3

The Word, Christ—"the same"—was in the beginning with God. That's John's beautifully expressed effort to convince us still further.

Christ was not merely in the mind of the Father at Creation —"in the beginning"—He was *there.* In fact, He was so *present* that John could state unequivocally that "all things were made *by him;* without him was not any thing made that was made."

Jesus Christ, the Creator? I certainly don't have skill enough with words or enough knowledge or understanding to explain *how* He could have been, but if I believe what these verses say, I know He was. *"All things were made by him; and without him was not any thing made that was made."* That includes us and it also includes the first spin of the earth and every other planet in every other system of planets and every star and every tulip and apple and hickory nut and rabbit and robin and gum tree and rose and berry and pine cone and puppy and green wave and sandy beach. And that first spin of the earth by His hand is still bringing both first light and sunset.

"Without him was not any thing made that was made."

St. John's Gospel is beautiful literature, but, to me, these sentences ring with a singular authenticity. No one else tried quite what John tried here—to hand us the shining key in the simplest, most usable way. No wonder God anointed his pen that day!

Repeat aloud to yourself: ". . . without him was not any thing made that was made." The words alone—the lay of one against the other—is all joy. But think, *think* what John is saying.

We can trust the Creator God because we know that Jesus can be trusted by anyone. Jesus isn't merely vouching for God's good will, He came to demonstrate that good will in a human body that people could touch. John, "the beloved disciple," touched Him. John, to me, touched Him in a special way—with his hands, his head on Jesus' shoulder, yes—but John was also chosen to be the writer who gives us this *one shining key to faith.*

I am not an academic theologian, not an "accredited" Bible scholar, but I am a *witness* to the fact that the moment in which a human faith grasps the Oneness of God and Jesus, "all things become new."

Can't those of us who hold this shining key paraphrase what John wrote? "Without him was not any thing made *new* that was made new."

"And the Word was made flesh, and dwelt among us . . ."

St. John 1:14

A footnote in an old, worn Bible my mother gave me right after my conversion to Jesus Christ in 1949 declares that the better translation of Jesus' greeting to Mary Magdalene and the other women on the morning He walked out of His tomb was not "All hail!" but "O joy!" Whichever it was, my heart wants to cry "O joy!" when I read John 1:14: "And the Word was made flesh, and dwelt among us."

I can imagine no other way God could have made His nature or His intentions clear. I've often been labeled Christocentric. That's fine with me, although some of the learned gentlemen who call me that don't mean it in an approving way. I simply know that I would not be a Christian at all if I had not come to believe that God bothered to become one of us. How else can we be sure that He means us well?

Throughout human history, until Jesus came, people could only stumble along following half-truths because God, remote and awesome as viewed in law or history or nature, was beyond knowing. The Old Testament is filled with stories of sincere people who tried as hard as they could to obey this overwhelming Jehovah. But until Jesus came to show us that there is no difference between Him and the Father, that He and the Father *are one and the same* in love, in compassion, in wisdom, in understanding, in creative and redeeming power, *who could be sure?*

His coming gave full content to the word "identification."

He got into human life with us. We can *know* now, beyond the shadow of any doubt. God stopped speaking from the "Jew's dark mountain top" and came into the world to show us *in Person* that what He really longs for is to "love and save and free us."

Is it any wonder that our sense of relief at the first realization spills directly over into joy?

Is it any wonder that, on that first Easter morning, Jesus cried, "O Joy! O Joy!"